101 Days Out
in Northern Ireland

Alf McCreary

LAGAN BOOKS

Published in 2006 for
Lagan Books
by
Appletree Press Ltd
The Old Potato Station
14 Howard Street South
Belfast
BT7 1AP

Tel: + 44 (0) 28 90 24 30 74
Fax: + 44 (0) 28 90 24 67 56
Email: reception@appletree.ie
Web-site: www.appletree.ie

A catalogue record for this book is available from the British Library.

101 Days Out in Northern Ireland

ISBN-10: 0 86281 855 9
ISBN-13: 978 0 86281 855 5

Desk & Marketing Editor: Jean Brown
Editorial work: Jim Black and Katell de Quelen
Designer: Stuart Wilkinson
Production Manager: Paul McAvoy

9 8 7 6 5 4 3 2 1

AP3322

CONTENTS

ABOUT THE AUTHOR

Alf McCreary is an award-winning journalist and author who lives and works in Belfast. He is an honours graduate of Queen's University, with a degree in Modern History. He has written countless articles and more than 30 books. His recent publications include *St Patrick's City – the Story of Armagh*, published in 2001 by the Blackstaff Press, and *Nobody's Fool*, the biography of the Church of Ireland Primate Archbishop Robin Eames, published by Hodder and Stoughton, in London. He is currently the Religion Correspondent of the *Belfast Telegraph* and has written a series of acclaimed travel books.

PUBLISHER'S NOTE

Every effort has been made to provide accurate information in this publication but opening hours and facilities can vary from those shown and are not guaranteed. To avoid disappointment readers are advised to check opening hours, prices and facilities with locations before travelling. Local tourist information centres are given as a point of contact for some towns and regions. Facility symbols, addresses and contact details etc. apply to the tourist information centres in these cases, unless otherwise stated.

The publisher would like to thank all the organisations whose kind assistance made this project possible.

It has given me much pleasure to compile this guide book to some of the most interesting places to visit and things to do in Northern Ireland. After so many years of 'the Troubles', it is wonderful to be able to draw attention to so many of these attractions, old and new, and to underline the rich historical and cultural heritage of the Province and its people.

The following list, which has been compiled with the assistance of colleagues at Appletree Press, is by no means definitive – nor is it meant to be. Inevitably some sights and activities have been omitted, inadvertently or by choice, and other people may have their own favourites, as well as those which have been included.

The main purpose of this publication is to provide the reader with a concise guide to some of the best activities and attractions available, and also to record the important facts about the facilities, such as the opening times and other appropriate details which are essential for an enjoyable visit.

It is my hope that the reader will learn as much in experiencing, as I have done in compiling, this list of a rich legacy which everyone can share. In conclusion I would like to thank my editor Jean Brown and also Jim Black at Appletree for their assistance in all the research, editing and production of this publication.

Alf McCreary MBE

Admission Charged

 Free Admission

 Parking

 No Parking

 Restaurant or Café on-site

 No on-site Restaurant or Café

 Toilet Facilities

 No Toilet Facilities

COUNTY ANTRIM

The small town of Antrim has a number of visitor attractions ranging from 17th-century gardens and an Arts Centre, to a first-class golf course and access to the largest inland lake in the British Isles. It is also the birthplace of Dr Alexander Irvine, author one of the most highly regarded books in local literature. (See Chimney Corner Cottage on page 23.)

One of the best ways of discovering the history of the area is to follow the Antrim Heritage Trail, which is well signposted and takes about 90 minutes to complete. It begins at the 19th-century Clotworthy Arts Centre and leads to the impressively restored Antrim Castle Gardens, one of the earliest of their kind still functional in the British Isles. The Trail also takes the visitor to the Long Canal and past the Round Pond to an old Burial Ground and Motte, and eventually to the remains of a 17th-century Castle, with its Barbican Gate and the arms of the former landlords, the Massereene family.

On the way to Lough Neagh the road winds past Massereene Golf Club, where the challenging 18-hole course is one of the finest in Ireland, and on to the Lough Shore Marina. This is a centre for water-based activities: or you might prefer feeding the many wild birds (including swans) on the shore, or just enjoying the beautiful scenery at the edge of the Lough.

Where is it?
Antrim Information Centre
16 High Street
Antrim
Co. Antrim
BT41 4AN

Who do I contact?
Tel: 028 9442 8331
Fax: 028 9448 7844
Email: info@antrim.gov.uk
Website: www.antrim.gov.uk

What do I need to know?
Antrim Information Centre is open all year but opening times vary according to season. As a general guide the Centre is open Monday to Friday from 9.00am to 5.00pm. In May, June and September the Centre also opens on Saturday from 10.00am to 1.00pm. In July and August, opening times from Monday to Friday are 9.00am to 5.30pm and on Saturday from 10.00am to 3.00pm. The Centre is closed on Sunday. Wheelchair accessible. Giftshop. Other services include accommodation booking, fishing licences and permits.

ANTRIM COAST ROAD

The Antrim Coast Road, travelling northwards from Larne to Ballycastle, is an area of outstanding natural and coastal beauty. Just outside Larne is Carnfunnock Country Park, which has nearly 191 hectares of gardens, walking trails and mixed woodland, as well as a 9-hole golf course and a touring caravan and camp site. There is a Visitor Centre with a gift and coffee shop, tourist information and a miniature railway for all ages. Carnfunnock also has an attractive walled garden with sundials, and a unique maze in the shape of Northern Ireland. The Park provides spectacular views of the coastline and lots of family activities.

The Antrim Coast Road itself was constructed between 1823-42 and replaced an often treacherous previous route. The Coast Road, with its tricky bends, winds along the rugged shoreline of the Irish Sea, and it also passes some of the superb scenery of the Glens of Antrim.

On a good day the coast of Scotland is clearly visible, and on a bad day, drivers need to keep a watch for possible rock falls, as well as other traffic. The road passes through quaint villages and small towns, and a good stopping-place for refreshment is the Londonderry Arms at Carnlough. This hotel was once owned by Sir Winston Churchill. At Cushendun there are historic cottages designed by the famous architect Clough Williams-Ellis, and further north near Ballycastle, the Ballypatrick Forest Park is worth visiting.

Where is it?
Larne Tourist Information Centre
Narrow Gauge Road
Larne
Co. Antrim
BT40 1XB

Who do I contact?

Tel: 028 2826 0088
Fax: 028 2826 0088
Email: larnetourism@btconnect.com

For further information on Carnfunnock Country Park please contact:
Tel: 028 2827 0541 (In season) *OR*
    028 2826 0088 (Out of season)
Fax: 028 2827 0852
Email: carnfunnock@btconnect.com
Website: www.larne.gov.uk/carnfunnock.html

What do I need to know?

Larne Tourist Information Centre is open all year, October to Easter from Monday to Friday between 9.00am and 5.00pm, Bank Holidays from 10.00am to 4.00pm. From Easter to September the Centre is open between 9.00am and 5.00pm, and on Saturday and Bank Holidays between 9.00am and 5.00pm. The Centre is closed on Sunday. Wheelchair access and Bureau de Change. Carnfunnock Country Park is open daily year-round except for Christmas Day and New Year's Day. During Spring and Summer the Park opens from 9.00am to dusk, and in July and August it opens between 9.00am and 9.00pm. Autumn and Winter opening hours are between 9.00am and 4.30pm. Entrance to the Park is free, but there is a charge for parking and activities. For school groups there is a Biodiversity Trail, a wildlife garden, a maths trail within the Walled Garden and orienteering. Schools and other groups should book their visit in advance.

Ballance House near Glenavy is a restored early-19th century farmhouse, and the birthplace of John Ballance, the Prime Minister of New Zealand from 1891-93. The son of a tenant farmer, he was the eldest of eleven children and was born in 1839. After leaving school at 14, he became a hardware- and ironmongery apprentice in Belfast. Ballance later went to Birmingham, and eventually emigrated to New Zealand with his ailing wife Fanny, whose brother lived there.

Sadly, the climate did not improve her health, and she died in 1868 – only five years after her marriage to Ballance. In 1870 he married Ellen Anderson, born in Ulster and the daughter of an English army officer. They had no children, and adopted the second Mrs Ballance's niece Kathleen.

John Ballance established the *Evening Herald* newspaper, later the *Wanganui Herald* and also became a successful politician. He held several ministerial portfolios before becoming Liberal Prime Minister. He was acclaimed as the architect of the welfare state, and was instrumental in giving the vote to women, a world first. His success with the economy also earned him the name 'The Rainmaker'.

Ballance House, which is easily accessible from Belfast and Antrim, has a wide range of exhibitions and audio-visual presentations, and a library.

Where is it?
118A Lisburn Road
Glenavy
Co. Antrim
BT29 4NT

Who do I contact?
Tel: 028 9264 8492
Fax: 028 9264 8098
Email: ballancenz@aol.com
Website: www.ballance.utvinternet.com

What do I need to know?
Open from April to September every Wednesday, Sunday and Bank Holiday (except 12th July), from 2.00pm-5.00pm. Ballance House can be visited at other times by arrangement. Group visits can be arranged by contacting 028 9258 7958. Afternoon teas can be provided for group visitors in the Tea Barn if booked in advance. For groups larger than 20, there is a reduced charge for the House tour. Part of the museum is housed upstairs. Disabled toilet and access to most areas. For information on forthcoming events at Ballance House please visit the website or see local press for details.

BALLYCASTLE

Ballycastle, near the northern tip of County Antrim, is a small and attractive town set in a region of great coastal beauty.

It is a lively market centre, which is situated at the foot of Glenshesk and Glentaisie. To the east is the rugged and impressive Fair Head, and the historic and unique Rathlin Island is only a 40-minute boat trip across the channel.

Near the harbour is a monument to Guglielmo Marconi and his assistants George Kemp and Edward Granville, who in 1898 set up a wireless telegraphy link between Ballycastle and Rathlin to prove for Lloyd's of London that such a link was possible. Unfortunately, during preparatory work, Mr Granville fell off a cliff and died. Though the wireless transmission was successful, the commercial potential for radio transmission was not pursued for some time. Ballycastle Museum holds material relating to Marconi's work and a remarkable collection of work created during the Arts and Crafts Movement in the Ireland dating from the early 1900s.

On the last Monday and Tuesday in August each year Ballycastle stages the famous two-day 'Oul Lammas Fair', which attracts many thousands of visitors to sample the local delights of 'dulse' (edible seaweed) and 'Yellowman' a hard, candy-like treat. Dating from the early-17th century, the Fair also attracts a wide range of stallholders, as well as sheep and pony breeders. It is great 'craic'.

Near Ballycastle the inter-denominational Corrymeela Centre on its high cliff-top is worth a visit from the ecumenically-minded. The nearby ruins of the 16th-century Franciscan Bonamargy Friary contain the remains of a local chieftain Sorley Boy McDonnell and the 17th-century recluse Julia McQuillan, also known as the 'Black Nun.' Overall, Ballycastle is a lively centre and an ideal base for touring the Glens and the North Antrim coast.

Where is it?
Ballycastle Tourist Information Centre
Sheskburn House
7 Mary Street
Ballycastle
Co. Antrim
BT54 6QH

Who do I contact?
Tel: 028 2076 2024
Fax: 028 2076 2515
Email: fcampbell@moyle-council.org
Website: www.moyle-council.org

What do I need to know?
Ballycastle Tourist Information Centre is open during July and August from Monday to Friday from 9.30am until 7.00pm, on Saturday from 10.00am until 6.00pm and on Sunday from 2.00pm until 6.00pm. The Centre is open from September to June on Monday to Friday between 9.30am and 5.00pm. There is a giftshop at the Centre. Disabled access. Ballycastle Museum is open daily during July and August from 12.00 noon until 6.00pm or by arrangement. Admission is free. Please contact the Museum on 028 2076 2942 for further information.

BALLYMENA

Ballymena is a prosperous market town, and a good base for visiting a wide range of historical sites in the area. It is particularly associated with, among others, Timothy Eaton who learned the drapery business in nearby Portglenone and emigrated to Canada in the 19th century, to found the famous chain of Eaton's department stores. It is said that thousands of Ulster people, who went to make a new life in Canada, were given their first job in Eaton's.

Ballymena has much of the character of an older market town but it is an excellent shopping centre, with the modern and impressive Fairhill and The Tower Centre. West of Ballymena is the beautiful village of Gracehill, with its historic Moravian Church and its graveyard where men are buried along one side, and women along the other.

Ballymena is within a short driving distance of Slemish, where St Patrick is said to have herded animals during his captivity in Ireland. In Ballymoney, to the north of Ballymena, there is a Memorial Garden to a modern hero, the former champion motorcyclist Joey Dunlop, who was tragically killed in 2000, during a race in Estonia. Ballymena is also the site of the *ecos millennium environmental centre*, which features educational displays on environmental issues.

Where is it?
Ballymena Tourist Information Centre
76 Church Street
Ballymena
Co. Antrim
BT43 6DF

Who do I contact?
Tel: 028 2563 8494
Fax: 028 2563 8495
Email: tourist.information@ballymena.gov.uk
Website: www.ballymena.gov.uk

What do I need to know?

Ballymena Tourist Information Centre is open all year, Monday to Friday from 9.00am to 5.00pm, and on Saturday from 10.00am to 4.00pm. In July and August, opening times from Monday to Friday are 9.00am to 5.30pm and on Saturday from 10.00am to 4.00pm. The Centre is closed on Sunday. Disabled access, with a low counter and a loop system for the hard of hearing. Giftshop. There is a photo/fax service, and an out-of-hours media information service. There is a museum nearby. The Information Centre will move to the Town Hall in late 2007.

CARRICK-A-REDE ROPE BRIDGE

The Carrick-a-Rede Rope Bridge, in the care of the National Trust and just north of Ballycastle, connects the mainland to the small Carrick Island. It was originally constructed to help fishermen gain swift access to the island in their pursuit of the offshore salmon, but it has also become a seasonal challenge to many visitors with a head for heights and an ability to ignore the Atlantic Ocean swirling below.

The crossing is not as daunting as it seems, but nevertheless visitors need to exercise due care, and also to wear appropriate clothing and footwear. (The bridge is not the best place for high-fashion shoes or stiletto heels!) Those who successfully make the return journey will be rewarded with spectacular views and a sense of achievement.

Not far away is the picturesque harbour of Ballintoy, with a lovely Church of Ireland building perched on the hill far above, as well as a remarkable house created by the eccentric genius Newton Penprase. Ballintoy itself is associated with the 18th-century landlord Downing Fullerton whose family name is perpetuated in Downing College, Cambridge and Downing Street, London.

On the way north to the famous Giant's Causeway, there are spectacular views of Whitepark Bay, and the tiny village of Portbraddan, which has arguably the world's smallest church – dedicated to St Gobhan. The road passes Dunseverick, once the capital of the ancient Kingdom of Dalriada.

Where is it?
119a White Park Road
Ballintoy
Ballycastle
Co. Antrim
BT54 6LS

Who do I contact?
Tel: 028 2076 9839 *OR*
     028 2073 1582
Fax: 028 2076 9839
Email: carrickarede@nationaltrust.org.uk
Website: www.ntni.org.uk

What do I need to know?
The Carrick-a-Rede Rope Bridge can be visited, weather permitting, every day during March to October from 10.00am until 6.00pm (and 7.00pm during July and August). Last tickets are sold 45 minutes before closing. Discounts are available for groups of 15 or more. Educational tours can be

arranged but must be booked in advance on 028 2076 9839. Children under ten receive a free 'Discovery' leaflet. There is a Millennium Path providing disabled access but due to steep slopes and many steps not all areas are accessible. Please wear suitable clothing and footwear.

Carrickfergus is an historic town situated on the shore of Belfast Lough. It is much older than Belfast: its history began in the sixth century, when it was established by Fergus of Ulster, who was king of Dalriada in Scotland. The town has many layers of history, including its magnificent Castle, (mentioned separately). The Gasworks, constructed between 1855-1965, is one of only three such sites surviving in the United Kingdom. It has the largest set of horizontal retorts in western Europe.

Located in the heart of the town, the new Carrickfergus Museum explores centuries of history through a range of fascinating collections which are being displayed in their home town for the first time. The museum reflects both the stories and experiences of ordinary people and also the dramatic and tumultuous events in the town's distinguished history. The museum has a permanent display gallery, temporary exhibition gallery, education and community room and a community archive.

The local Gasworks Preservation Society, in association with the Environment and Heritage Service, has beautifully restored the formerly dilapidated buildings and plant. Visitors can find out how the gas was made from coal, and learn about its practical application, as well as the future of natural gas. The FLAME facility also presents an historic exhibition of appliances and a library on the industry.

Other attractions in Carrickfergus include the 12th-century St Nicholas' Church with its fine stained-glass and 'crooked' aisle where the poet Louis MacNeice's father was rector, and the Andrew Jackson and U.S. Rangers' Centre at Boneybefore, just to the north. This includes the reconstruction of an 18th-century cottage on the site of the ancestral home of the seventh President of the USA. The American Army Rangers unit was formed here in 1942. During July and August weekends there are regular events here, featuring craftwork and rural life.

Where is it?
Carrickfergus Tourist Information Centre
Carrickfergus Museum and Civic Centre
11 Antrim Street
Carrickfergus
Co. Antrim
BT38 7DG

Who do I contact?
For further information on Carrickfergus please contact Carrickfergus Museum and Tourist Information Centre:
Tel: 028 9335 8049
Fax: 028 9335 0350
Email: touristinfo@carrickfergus.org
Website: www.carrickfergus.org

For further information on FLAME please contact:
Tel: 028 9336 9575
Email: info@flamegasworks.fsnet.co.uk
Website: www.flamegasworks.co.uk

For further information on Andrew Jackson and U.S. Rangers'
Centre please contact:
Tel: 028 9335 8049

What do I need to know?

Carrickfergus Museum and Tourist Information Centre is open all year from Monday to Friday between 9.00am and 6.00pm and on Saturday from 10.00am to 6.00pm. Open on Sunday from April to September between 1.00pm and 6.00pm. Disabled access. The museum has a giftshop, a Tourist Information desk and a café. An education and community room is available for schools and other groups who should book their visit in advance. The FLAME Gaswork Museum is open by appointment only from January to March, on Sunday in April and October between 2.00pm and 5.00pm, and Sunday to Friday from May to September between 2.00pm and 5.00pm. Disabled access. Andrew Jackson and U.S. Rangers' Centre is open from Monday to Friday from April to September between 10.00am and 6.00pm, and on Saturday and Sunday between 2.00pm and 6.00pm. For further information on forthcoming events in the Carrickfergus area please visit the websites or see local press for details.

Carrickfergus Castle is a superbly maintained 12th-century Anglo-Norman structure, which is one of the best of its kind still in existence. Its silhouette dominates the broad entrance to Belfast Lough.

The Castle was built by John de Courcy, the Earl of Ulster from 1180-1204, and it was fought over by successive warlords, chieftains and invaders. It was captured by a daring French fleet in the mid-18th century, and in 1788 the buccaneer American Paul Jones sailed up Belfast Lough and past the Castle to capture *HMS Drake*.

The Castle, which is maintained by the Government's Environment and Heritage Service, is open to the public, and the exhibits are well displayed. A number of life-size models also bring to life part of the Castle's history. Guided tours are available, and pre-booking is essential for larger tours. There is a Visitor Centre at the entrance, with a gift shop and a refreshment area, and information booklets are on sale. Special events are staged throughout the year, including the Lughnasa Fair during the last weekend of July. The Castle can be hired for a range of events, and the vaults are available for children's parties.

Outside the Castle, there is the diminutive life-size statue of the famous King William III, who landed at Carrickfergus at the start of his 17th-century Irish campaign to secure the Protestant succession to the British throne. Nearby is a plaque commemorating the visit of a modern monarch – Queen Elizabeth II – in 1961.

Where is it?
Carrickfergus Castle
Marine Highway
Carrickfergus
Co. Antrim
BT38 7BG

Who do I contact?
Tel: 028 9335 1273
Fax: 028 9336 5190
Website: www.ehsni.gov.uk

What do I need to know?
Open all year, but opening times vary. During the winter months (October to March) the castle is open Monday to Saturday 10.00am to 4.00pm, Sunday 2.00pm to 4.00pm. April, May and September opening times are Monday to Saturday 10.00am to 6.00pm, Sunday 2.00pm to 6.00pm. June, July and August opening times are Monday to Saturday 10.00am to 6.00pm, Sunday 12.00 noon to 6.00pm. Discounts are available for groups of 10 or more. Limited disabled access. Last admission to the castle is 30 minutes before closing. Schools and youth groups should book their visit in advance. There is a giftshop beside the entrance. For further information on forthcoming events, please visit the website or see local press for details.

CHIMNEY CORNER COTTAGE – POGUE'S ENTRY

The Chimney Corner Cottage at Pogue's Entry in Antrim is the well-preserved birthplace of Dr Alexander Irvine (1863-1941) whose book *My Lady of the Chimney Corner* is one of the most celebrated in Ulster literature. In it he tells the moving story of his mother Anna, an educated Catholic married to Jamie, an illiterate Protestant cobbler, who struggled to bring up their 12 children in abject poverty, at a time when 'mixed marriages' had their own particular challenges.

However, his mother's philosophy that "Love Is Enough" became the inspiration for Alexander Irvine's life and work. His colourful career included mining, the army and acting, as well as writing, academe and the Christian ministry. His various books provide vivid descriptions of life in the 19th century, and he eventually became the minister of the Church of the Ascension in New York's fashionable Fifth Avenue. He died in California, and in 1946 his ashes were brought to Antrim and interred beside his parents in the small graveyard of All Saints' Church.

The Chimney Corner Cottage was first opened to the public in 1934 and it is maintained by Antrim Borough Council as a tribute to Dr Irvine and his family, and as a reminder of the power of love despite the harshness of Irish life in days gone by.

Where is it?
Church Street
Antrim
Co. Antrim
BT41 4BA

Who do I contact?
For further information on Pogue's Entry and the Chimney Corner Cottage please contact Clotworthy Arts Centre:
Tel: 028 9448 1338
Fax: 028 9448 1344
Email: clotworthyarts@antrim.gov.uk
Website: www.antrim.gov.uk

What do I need to know?
Pogue's Entry is open during July and August on Thursday and Friday afternoon from 2.00pm to 5.00pm, and on Saturday from 10.00am to 5.00pm (closed 1.00pm to 2.00pm for lunch). Open at other times by arrangement. Disabled access.

DUNLUCE CASTLE

Dunluce Castle is a large and picturesque remnant of a 16th-17th century castle. It is thought to occupy the site of an earlier structure inhabited by the McQuillans of the Route. Dunluce Castle, like all similar fortifications in ancient Ireland, was fought over many times by many different armies and groups with vested political interests. In the mid-16th century it fell to the local MacDonnell Clan, whose most colourful leader Sorley Boy was later laid to rest at the Bonamargy Friary at Ballycastle.

Life at Dunluce Castle was dangerous enough, due to incessant wars and disputes, but its precarious perch on the edge of the cliff brought its own perils. On a stormy night in 1639, the kitchen servants and others were lost when part of the Castle toppled into the raging ocean beneath. Some time later the MacDonnells wisely decided to make their headquarters elsewhere, and following their withdrawal from Dunluce, the Castle gradually fell into disuse. However, it has been maintained in relatively good repair and is worth a visit not only for the superb views over the Causeway coast and seawards to Scotland, but also for its excellent photo opportunities.

Where is it?
Dunluce Castle
87 Dunluce Road
Bushmills
Co. Antrim
BT57 8UY

Who do I contact?
Tel: 028 2073 1938
Fax: 028 2073 2850
Email: dunluce.castle@doeni.gov.uk
Website: www.ehsni.gov.uk/places/monuments/dunluce.html

What do I need to know?
Open daily all year. Open during October to March from 10.00am until 5.00pm, April to September from 10.00am until 6.00pm from Monday-Saturday and 2.00pm to

6.00pm on Sunday. Last admission 30 minutes before closing. Guided tours are available for school and tour groups and should be booked in advance. Discounts are available for groups of ten and over. Limited disabled access throughout. Display area, with large replica model of castle. Giftshop on site. Dunluce Castle is sited beside the coast road (A2) between Bushmills and Portrush.

ECOS MILLENNIUM ENVIRONMENTAL CENTRE

The *ecos millennium environmental centre* at Ballymena is both a country park and nature reserve. It provides families and individuals with the opportunity to learn about and to explore environmental issues. This formerly derelict farmland has been developed into woodland, dry and wet grassland, ponds and a lake. They attract and sustain a wide variety of wildlife – including butterflies and dragonflies, as well as birds and many varieties of wildflowers.

There are about 5 miles of paths for walking, jogging and cycling, and there are marked routes along the river and attractive woodland. Dogs are welcome, but must be kept on a lead. There are also interactive zones where all the family can learn more about the environment.

There are opportunities to explore more closely the pond life in the lake, to discover how water, wind and heat are creating 'marble sculpture', and also to find out how the *ecos centre* generates electricity by means of wood, wind and sun.

Where is it?

ecos millennium environmental centre
Kernohans Lane
Broughshane Road
Ballymena
Co. Antrim
BT43 7QA

Who do I contact?

Tel: 028 2566 4400
Fax: 028 2563 8984
Email: info@ecoscentre.com
Website: www.ecoscentre.com

What do I need to know?

Opening hours vary according to season and it is advisable to check before travelling. As a general guide the *ecos centre* is open every Monday to Friday from 9.00am to 5.00pm, but closed Saturday and Sunday. During the summer season (June to August), the centre is open daily. There are guided tours by arrangement, for which there is a charge but group discounts are available. Educational activity packs are available for school groups and teachers should contact the Education Co-ordinator for further details on 028 2566 4404. All school and group visits should be booked in advance. Slemish market gardens are on site and a coffee shop is open during summer opening hours. Disabled access. The *ecos centre* can also be booked for conferences and catering is available for events on request. For details on opening hours or forthcoming events please visit the website or contact the centre directly.

The Giant's Causeway, on the North Antrim coast, has rightly been described as one of the eight wonders of the world. It is the subject of legends and folklore, but in reality it is a geological complex of small basalt columns and outcrops formed some 60 million years ago by the cooling of lava. The locals, however, have a much more colourful story, and the Giant's Causeway is traditionally a path built across the sea by the legendary Irish giant Finn McCool to do battle with his Scottish counterpart.

The Giant's Causeway, described somewhat unkindly by Dr Samuel Johnson in the 18th century as "worth seeing... but not worth going to see" is a major tourist attraction, and a UNESCO World Heritage site. There are outstanding views and challenging walks, as well as much geological history. One of the special attractions is the Port Cuan cave, accessible by boat. In past decades the guides blew bugles so that visitors could hear the dramatic echoes.

The site and paths are owned by the National Trust in association with Moyle District Council, which manages the Visitors Centre and the large car park nearby. The Centre provides an audio-visual presentation and commentaries in several languages, as well as souvenir shops, a tourist information area and a restaurant, and it is a good starting point for a visit. There is also the homely Causeway Hotel nearby. A bus is available to ferry visitors from the Centre down to the Grand Causeway.

Near the Causeway is Port na Spaniagh where a treasure trove, now in the Ulster Museum, was recovered in the late 1960s from the Spanish Armada vessel the *Girona*, which foundered off the Causeway Coast during a fierce storm in 1588. Not far from the Causeway car park is the Causeway Coast steam train to Bushmills, with period coaches and spectacular views.

Where is it?

Giant's Causeway Visitors' Centre
44 Causeway Road
Bushmills
Co. Antrim
BT57 8SU

Who do I contact?

To contact the National Trust at the Giant's Causeway:
Tel: 028 2073 1582 *OR*
     028 2073 2972
Fax: 028 2073 2963
Email: giantscauseway@nationaltrust.org.uk
Website: www.ntni.org.uk

To contact the Giant's Causeway Tourist Information Centre:
Tel: 028 2073 1855
Fax: 028 2073 2537
Email: info@giantscausewaycentre.com
Website: www.giantscausewaycentre.com

What do I need to know?

There is open access to the stones and coastal path year-round, except 25th and 26th December. Opening hours for the Trust shop and tea room may vary – please check before travelling. Guided tours of the Causeway are available.

School and other group visits should be booked in advance. Educational facilities are available and should be pre-booked on 028 2073 1582. Gift shop. Disabled access to most areas.

GLENARIFF FOREST PARK

Glenariff Forest Park in the heart of the beautiful Glens of Antrim is a popular tourist attraction for those who like bracing walks amid outstanding scenery. The 'Queen of the Glens', Glenariff is a steep U-shaped glacial valley, with hanging waterfalls over the upper, sheer edges. The Glenariff and Inver rivers run through Glenariff Forest's 1,182 hectares. The Forest Park was developed and opened for recreation in 1977. It contains a mixture of original tree and scrub species (such as oak, elm, hazel and ash) and other introduced tree species (beech, larch, Scots pine, Douglas fir and rhododendron). There are some mature stands of Larch, Spruce, Pine and Fir in Glenariff, some dating from 1921.

Glenariff Forest is home to many animals of conservation concern, most notably Red Squirrel, Hen Harrier and Irish Hare. Look out for the little white chested dipper birds in the river areas. The Forest Service aims to protect and enhance the Park's many important habitats, flora and fauna. Glenariff's population of Red Squirrels is protected from the introduced Grey Squirrel by the surrounding high moorland. The squirrels build their dreys (nests) close to the trunks high up in trees and the first litter of young squirrels (called kittens) arrives about March, often with a second litter in July.

The Park has several trails for visitors to enjoy. The Scenic Trail covering 8.9km is for some the most challenging. It leads down the Inver River gorge, nearly to the Ess-na-Crub Waterfall, then climbs steeply, with very fine views over the Glen and across the sea as far as the Mull of Kintyre. The spectacular 3km Waterfall Trail takes you through the Glenariff National Nature Reserve along the deep wooded gorge of the Glenariff River. Stairways and pathways are cut into the near vertical sides of the gorge past rapids and waterfalls; there are boardwalks on stilts in the river, and a spray-swept bridge at the very foot of the highest waterfall, Ess-na-Larach (Fall of Mare).

This rocky, moist and shady environment protects a rich diversity of ferns, mosses and liverworts, as well as a rare snail, the only place in Ulster where it exists. An optional detour on the Waterfall Walk, the 0.9km Rainbow Trail includes crossing the Rainbow Bridge. The short Viewpoint Trail covers 0.9km and provides excellent views over the Glenariff Glen to the sea. The trail passes the café and runs through the ornamental gardens to the car park. Also of interest is Portglenone Forest on the River Bann, where visitors can see acre upon acre of bluebells and other ancient woodland flora and follow riverside paths.

Where is it?
98 Glenariff Road
Glenariff
Co. Antrim
BT44 0QX

Who do I contact?

Tel: 028 2955 6000
Fax: 028 2955 7162
Email: customer.forestservice@dardni.gov.uk
Website: forestserviceni.gov.uk

What do I need to know?

Glenariff Forest Park is open daily year-round from 10.00am to 8.00pm. Disabled access. Giftshop. There is a Visitor Centre with an interactive display and exhibition, and also a shop and café.

IRISH LINEN CENTRE AND LISBURN MUSEUM

The recently-designated City of Lisburn was once part of a thriving Ulster linen trade, which was helped to develop in the district by 17th-century refugee French and Dutch Huguenots, who settled locally to escape religious persecution in Europe.

The history and importance of the linen industry is expertly recorded in the Irish Linen Centre exhibition, 'Flax to Fabric'. Located in Lisburn's original 17th-century market house, where 'brown linen' was sold, the exhibition provides a fascinating survey of part of Ulster's heritage. Visitors can see and talk to weavers working on 19th-century damask hand looms and can attempt the delicate skill of hand spinning.

As well as the 'Flax to Fabric' exhibition, the Museum also provides important information on the history of Lisburn and the Lagan Valley. It has a varied temporary exhibition programme of displays from its own collections and touring exhibitions of art and other topics of local interest. There is a reference library of material relevant to the study of the area's local history (including local newspapers covering the first half of the 20th century) and a specialised collection of material on the Irish linen industry. Both libraries can be consulted by prior arrangement. The Museum also holds a collection of old photographs of the district.

Where is it?
Market Square
Lisburn
Co. Antrim
BT28 1AG

Who do I contact?
Tel: 028 9266 3377
Fax: 028 9267 2624
Email: irishlinencentre@lisburn.gov.uk
Website: www.lisburncity.gov.uk/irish_linen_centre_and_
　　　　　lisburn_museum

What do I need to know?
Open daily (except on Sunday) from 9.30am to 5.00pm. Workshops and guided tours are available for school groups if booked in advance. Parking for disabled drivers. Disabled access throughout, with a loop system for the hard of hearing. Baby changing facilities. The Museum shop sells a wide range of linens, books and craftworks. Café Crommelin is licensed. For further information on forthcoming events at

ANTRIM

the Irish Linen Centre and Lisburn Museum please visit the website or see local press for details.

The Old Bushmills Distillery, situated in the small town of Bushmills on the North Antrim coast, is the world's oldest licensed whiskey distillery. Its colourful history began in 1608 when the original licence was granted to Sir Thomas Phillips, a local landowner, by the English King James I to distil *Aqua Vitae* – literally the 'water of life'.

The Old Bushmills Distillery has being doing this expertly ever since, and it produces one of the world's most acclaimed whiskeys, with connoisseurs sampling its distinctive taste all over the globe. The Distillery itself with its pagoda towers has a beautiful setting. It is close to the fabled Causeway Coast with its historic ruins like Dunluce Castle, its long, clean beaches, its outstanding golf courses, and the fabled Giant's Causeway itself.

Old Bushmills has a busy Visitor Centre, which provides a comprehensive outline of its history, and also tours of the Distillery, as well as an opportunity to sample and purchase this unique Irish whiskey.

Where is it?
2 Distillery Road
Bushmills
Co. Antrim
BT57 8XH

Who do I contact?
Tel: 028 2073 3218
Fax: 028 2073 1339
Website: www.bushmills.com

What do I need to know?
The Distillery is open daily year-round, but is closed on Good Friday, 12th of July, Christmas and New Year holidays. Please telephone for guided tour details including admission charges and any holiday closures. Groups of 15 or more should be booked in advance. Smoking is not permitted anywhere in the Distillery. Children under seven are welcome but are not permitted on the guided tour. There is no wheelchair access to the Distillery Tour, but all other areas are accessible. The restaurant and giftshop are open during normal visiting hours and can be visited without charge.

PATTERSON'S SPADE MILL

Patterson's Spade Mill is a National Trust property situated at Templepatrick on the main Belfast-Antrim Road. It can also been glimpsed from the M2 motorway when travelling north.

Once owned by the Patterson family, it is the last water-driven spade mill in daily use within the British Isles. John Patterson was the fourth generation of the family involved in spade-making when he moved from Tyrone to Templepatrick shortly after the First World War to take advantage of the good water supply to produce power from turbines. Happily, the tradition has been carried on, and today the Mill employs two spade-makers. Visitors can still sample all the main stages (and noises) involved in the production process.

There is an exhibition in the reception area, and guided tours are available. Handcrafted spades are on sale and also made to particular specifications. A visit to Patterson's Spade Mill will bring back all the flavour of life in the industrial age with the smell of oil, metal and wood, and also the clangour of hammers, turbines and presses.

Where is it?
751 Antrim Road
Templepatrick
Co. Antrim
BT39 0AP

Who do I contact?
Tel: 028 9443 3619
Email: pattersons@nationaltrust.org.uk
Website: www.ntni.org.uk

What do I need to know?
The Mill is open at weekends during April, May and September, between 2.00pm and 6.00pm. Open daily during Easter holiday week between 2.00pm and 6.00pm. From the beginning of June to the end of August, the Mill is open from Tuesday to Sunday between 2.00pm and 6.00pm. Disabled

access. There are hands-on activities and a children's guide for school and youth groups, who should book their visit in advance. There are group discounts available. The last admission is one hour before closing.

PORTRUSH

Portrush on the North Antrim coast is one of the main seaside resorts in Northern Ireland with numerous attractions for visitors, and particularly for families. It is set in an area of great natural beauty, with excellent beaches including the long White Rocks strand, and the world-class Royal Portrush Golf Course.

The town has been traditionally a 'bucket-and-spade' resort, but like nearly all others in the British Isles it has adapted well to changing circumstances and the needs of today's discerning travellers.

Waterworld in Portrush has become a major family attraction, with its inter-active water playground for children, and ten-pin bowling facility. The long-established Barry's Amusements centre has been popular with generations of visitors, and it still has much to offer, as has the Dunluce Centre. This is a large family-entertainment complex at the heart of the town.

Portrush itself has moved upmarket in recent years, with attractive property and good restaurants. It is an ideal base for a relaxed holiday and for sampling some of the many tourist delights of the North Coast, including the nearby Giant's Causeway and the Old Bushmills Distillery, and the superb coastal scenery as far as Ballycastle and beyond.

Where is it?
Tourist Information Centre
Dunluce Centre
10 Sandhill Drive
Portrush
Co. Antrim
BT56 8DF

Who do I contact?
Tel: 028 7082 3333
Fax: 028 7082 1358
Email: portrushtic@btconnect.com
Website: www.colerainebc.gov.uk

What do I need to know?
The Tourist Information Office is open from March to October. Open daily from April to June, and September, from Monday to Friday between 9.00am and 5.00pm and at weekends from 12.00 noon to 5.00pm. Open daily during July and August between 9.00am and 7.00pm. During March and October the Office is open at weekends from 12.00 noon to 5.00pm. Disabled access. Giftshop. A café and toilets are available during regular Dunluce Centre opening hours.

Rathlin Island is a unique location for tourists and visitors who seek rugged beauty, abundant birdlife and wildlife, and sites of historical interest. Still inhabited, it was once relatively remote across the dangerous six-mile channel, which separates it from the mainland. Today, however, it is accessible by means of a regular modern ferry, but on occasions the crossing can still be challenging for non-sailors.

One of the best sites for birdwatching in Europe is the Bull Point where many thousands of seabirds congregate, particularly in mid-summer. Return transport from the ferry by coach is available, though if time is not a problem, the first (or return) part of the journey can be made on foot. The terrain is not difficult, the views are rewarding and in season there is a wide range of plants and wild-flowers, as well as the unforgettable sound of lark-song.

There are several ancient sites ranging from Mesolithic times (6000 BC) and also the cave where the exiled Robert the Bruce is said to have watched a spider repeatedly try to reach the roof by its thread. This inspired him to 'try, try again', and motivated him to return to Scotland where he eventually defeated his enemies. Rathlin has modern facilities including a restaurant and pub, overnight accommodation including the National Trust's Manor House, and a Boathouse Visitors Centre. There is also a small Catholic chapel, a beautifully restored Church of Ireland building and a graveyard with fascinating headstones near the shoreline.

Where is it?
Island 6 miles off north Antrim coast from Ballycastle. A ferry service (for which there is a charge), is offered by Caledonian MacBrayne and leaves from Ballycastle Harbour.

Who do I contact?
For further information on Rathlin Island please contact Ballycastle Tourist Information Centre:
Tel: 028 2076 2024
Fax: 028 2076 2515
Email: tourism@moyle-council.org
Website: www.moyle-council.org

For further information on staying at the Manor House on Rathlin Island please contact:
Tel: 028 2076 3964
Fax: 028 2076 3964

For further information on the Caledonian MacBrayne ferry services to Rathlin Island please contact:
Tel: 028 2076 9299
Fax: 028 2076 9298
Website: www.calmac.co.uk/rathlin

What do I need to know?
Ballycastle Tourist Information Centre is open during July and August from Monday to Friday between 9.30am and 7.00pm, on Saturday from 10.00am until 6.00pm and on Sunday from 2.00pm until 6.00pm. The Centre is open Monday to Friday from September to June between 9.30am and 5.00pm. There is a giftshop at the

Centre. Disabled access. The Manor House is open year-round and offers bed and breakfast accommodation. Its Brockley tea room is open to guests and visitors.

SENTRY HILL

Sentry Hill in Newtownabbey is a fascinating example of an historic Ulster farmhouse, which has been carefully preserved to give an insight into the rural life of the 19th and early-20th century.

It was the home of the Scottish McKinney family who emigrated to Ireland in the early-18th century, and a great many of its contents have been preserved intact. William Fee McKinney was born in 1832 and spent virtually his lifetime at Sentry Hill. He was a dedicated collector of family memorabilia and other artefacts, and also an accomplished early photographer. Due to his tireless endeavours, much of particular historical interest has been preserved about life at Sentry Hill and those of its inhabitants and their many guests. Dr Joe Dundee, the grandson of William McKinney, was a noted racehorse breeder and trainer. He took over Sentry Hill in the 1930s, and lived there from his retirement in 1977 until his death nearly 20 years later.

Sentry Hill offers an introductory video and guided tours, as well as an Exhibition Gallery, a Resource Room with computers, a refreshment and gift area, and an informal garden.

Where is it?

Sentry Hill
40 Ballycraigy Road
Newtownabbey
Co. Antrim
BT36 8SX

Who do I contact?

Tel: 028 9083 2363
Textphone: 028 9084 2517
Email: sentry.hill@btconnect.com
Website: www.newtownabbey.gov.uk

What do I need to know?

Please check for details of guided tours and opening times. As a general guide, Sentry Hill is open April to June and September from Tuesday to Sunday between 2.00pm and 5.00pm, and on Bank Holidays from 11.00am to 5.00pm. The last tour takes place at 3.45pm. Opening times during July and August are Tuesday to Saturday between 10.30am and 5.30pm, on Sunday from 2.00pm to 5.30pm and on Bank Holidays from 10.30am to 5.30pm. The last tour takes place at 4.15pm. Sentry Hill is closed on the 12th of July. Disabled access to the farmhouse is limited to the ground floor, but a virtual tour of the upper floors is available in the Visitor Centre. Giftshop. Guided tours are available to school and youth groups, who should book their visit in advance. A school visit combines a tour of Sentry Hill farmhouse with a 'hands-on' workshop focusing on Victorian costume and artifacts. There is a discount for groups larger than 10 by arrangement. Young people aged 16 and under should be accompanied by an adult on guided tours.

Slemish Mountain near Ballymena is the plug over a medium-sized extinct volcano, where St Patrick is said to have spent six years as a slave herding animals. Though Ireland's patron saint did not make the location clear in his autobiographical *Confessio*, there is a pilgrimage each St Patrick's Day to the 180-metre summit.

The circular climb is steep and rocky in parts, but the views over the Antrim countryside and even as far as Scotland are worth the effort. Climbers are advised to use the marked route, and to equip themselves with all-weather clothing and stout footwear. There is an interpretive centre at the start of the walk, and also toilets, but at present there are no catering facilities. Slemish is best reached by road from the attractive village of Broughshane, which is also known as 'the Garden Village of Ulster'.

Where is it?
Slemish: from Ballymena take A42 for Broughshane. Turn right in the village (B94). Slemish is signposted from there.

Who do I contact?
For further information on Slemish please contact Ballymena Tourist Centre:
Tel: 028 2563 8494
Fax: 028 2563 8495
Email: tourist.information@ballymena.gov.uk
Website: www.ballymena.gov.uk

What do I need to know?

Access to the summit is available all year round. Disabled access at the foot of Slemish and toilets. Picnic facilities are available. CCTV is in operation.

T.A.C.T. WILDLIFE CENTRE

The T.A.C.T. (Talnotry Avian Care Trust) is a Charitable Trust and a Wildlife Centre run by volunteers in the village of Crumlin. Its role is to rehabilitate sick or abandoned wild birds and mammals. and to release them – when and where appropriate – to their natural environment. If an animal or bird cannot be released again or found a good home, it remains at the Centre for the rest of its life.

Wild birds, including swans, ducks, geese and others can be found in the 200-year-old Walled Garden. Other inhabitants of the Wildlife centre include sparrowhawks and owls as well as hedgehogs, rabbits, foxes, badgers and guinea-pigs. The Centre is open at set times, and visits outside these hours should be organised by arrangement. A small donation is requested on entry to help defray costs, as there is no Government funding for looking after the creatures.

Education is an important part of the focus of T.A.C.T., especially for the young and those with special needs, and the participation of the public, including the disabled and people from socially deprived backgrounds, is encouraged. Activities include 'hands-on' events with selected birds and animals.

Where is it?
Talnotry Avian Care Trust
2 Crumlin Road
Crumlin   Near Belfast (west)
Co. Antrim
BT29 4AD

Who do I contact?
Tel: 028 9442 2900
Fax: 028 9442 2900
Email: tactwildlife@btinternet.com
Website: www.tactwildlifecentre.org.uk

What do I need to know?
The Trust is open year-round from Monday to Friday between 12.00 noon and 3.00pm, and on Sunday between 2.00pm and 5.00pm. At other times, the Trust is open by arrangement only. Disabled access. Giftshop. There is a group discount available and schools and other groups should book their visit in advance. Environmental resources and audiovisual facilities are available. The Wildlife Centre backs on to Crumlin Glen where there is a picnic area and access to disabled toilets.

COUNTY ARMAGH

Ardress House is a National Trust property situated at Annaghmore, near Portadown. It was originally a 17th-century farmhouse but following the wedding of George Ensor to Sarah Clarke of Ardress, the House was enlarged with an extra wing and a wall with dummy windows.

The drawing room with the elegant stucco plasterwork by Michael Stapleton of Dublin, has four beautiful plaques which represent the different seasons. There is also a traditional farmyard. Admission is by guided tour and there are facilities – by arrangement – for group tours outside normal hours.

Other National Trust properties in the area include The Argory at the Moy, and Derrymore House in Bessbrook. A tour to all three is possible in the course of a day, as they are broadly in the same area of Co. Armagh.

Where is it?
64 Ardress Road
Annaghmore
Portadown
Co. Armagh
BT62 1SQ

Who do I contact?
Tel: 028 8778 4753 (The Argory)
Fax: 028 3885 1236
Email: ardress@nationaltrust.org.uk
Website: www.ntni.org.uk

What do I need to know?
Ardress House is open from April to September on Saturday and Sunday. House open from 2.00pm until 6.00pm with last admission 30 minutes before closing. Grounds are open daily all year round from dawn to dusk. Interpretations of life in Ardress House during visiting hours. School and other groups should book their visit in advance. Disabled access. Giftshop. Group discounts available.

THE ARGORY

The Argory is a National Trust property situated in the Moy area. This homely 18th-century mansion has remained largely unchanged since the early 1900s. It was built in 1824, and contains a delightful cabinet barrel-organ and fascinating Edwardian artefacts.

In the stable yard there is a harness room as well as horse-carriages, a laundry and a gas plant. The Argory also has beautiful gardens, and riverside and woodland walks. People should note that the house does not have electric light, and for the best viewing of the interior and its paintings, visitors should avoid overcast days when the natural light is limited.

Afternoon teas are available in Lady Ada's tea room, with home-baking a speciality. The house is suitable for school groups, and there is an education room, with hands-on facilities. Other National Trust properties in the area include the nearby Ardress House at Annaghmore, near Portadown, and Derrymore House at Bessbrook.

Where is it?
144 Derrycaw Road
Moy
Dungannon
Co. Armagh
BT71 6NA

Who do I contact?
Tel: 028 8778 4753
Fax: 028 8778 9598
Email: argory@nationaltrust.org.uk
Website: www.ntni.org.uk

What do I need to know?
Grounds open daily during May-September from 10.00am until 7.00pm and from October-April from 10.00am until 4.00pm. House opening hours vary with time of year and visitors are advised to check before travelling. As a general guide the house is open at weekends between 1.00pm-6.00pm from mid-March to May (with daily opening during Easter week). The house is open daily between 1.00pm-6.00pm during June, July and August and at weekends during September. Last admission one hour before closing. Facilities (including guided tours) are available for school groups, which should be booked in advance. There is disabled access throughout. Giftshop. Visitors should bear in mind that there is no electric lighting at The Argory.

The City of Armagh is one of the most fascinating historical centres in Ulster. It is the ecclesiastical capital of Ireland, where St Patrick established his first main church in 445 AD. Today the beautiful Protestant and Roman Catholic Cathedrals of St Patrick face each other on separate hills across the city, as continuing custodians of two differing main traditions of a shared Christianity. There are other noteworthy churches in Armagh, including several Presbyterian and other Church of Ireland establishments, as well as St Malachy's Chapel – named after a 12th-century Archbishop of Armagh who was a confidant of the Pope and a friend of St Bernard of Clairvaux.

Armagh City, which is actually a medium-sized town, has beautiful Georgian architecture, created by an entrepreneurial 18th-century Archbishop of Armagh: Richard Robinson, later Lord Rokeby. The Georgian Mall, with its green quadrangle of grass and trees, is particularly attractive, and up near the Protestant cathedral is a fine sweep of buildings known as Vicar's Hill. The end-house was the birthplace of Sir Charles Wood, the outstanding 19th-century composer of sacred works.

Armagh is replete with museums and heritage centres, which are listed individually in this publication. It also has the elegant and award-winning Market Place Theatre and Arts Centre. This location reflects a wide range of cultural events in a city which boasts such diverse talents as the Armagh Rhymers, maintaining a tradition going back 2,500 years, and the distinctive paintings of the internationally acclaimed artist J.B. Vallely.

Where is it?
Armagh Tourist Information Centre
40 English Street
Armagh
Co. Armagh
BT61 4BA

Who do I contact?
Tel: 028 3752 1800
Fax: 028 3752 8329
Email: info@visitarmagh.com
Website: www.visitarmagh.com

What do I need to know?
Armagh Tourist Information Centre is open year-round from Monday to Saturday between 9.00am and 5.30pm, and on Sunday between 2.00pm and 5.00pm. During June to August Sunday opening hours are extended to between 12.00 noon and 5.30pm. Disabled access and ramp. Giftshop. There is a touchscreen computer information kiosk with details on the East Border region and visitors can book accommodation through the Tourist Information Centre. Located beside St Patrick's Trian.

ARMAGH MUSEUMS

Strolling along the tree-lined Mall, near the centre of St Patrick's cathedral city, a visit to Armagh County Museum is an ideal way to experience a flavour of the orchard county. Built in 1834 to a Classical design, its impressive columns dominate the entrance, making it one of the most distinctive buildings in the area.

The Museum's extensive collections and displays reflect the lives of people who have lived and worked in Armagh or have been associated with the county. Discover a rich and varied legacy revealed in objects ranging from prehistoric artefacts to household items from a bygone age. There are military uniforms, wedding dresses, ceramics, natural history specimens and railway memorabilia. An impressive art collection includes works by many well-known Irish artists. The Museum also has an extensive reference library, rich in local archive material, along with photographic and map collections. With a range of changing exhibitions throughout the year, it is an ideal place to see and explore the fair county of Armagh.

Further along the Mall is the Royal Irish Fusiliers Museum, which tells the stirring tale of this once-famous British Regiment, which like many others, is now only a part of history. Its achievements in the pursuit of Empire, its participation in crucial campaigns nearer home and its outstanding record in two World Wars is faithfully recorded. A forerunner of this Regiment was the "Eagle Takers", the first group to capture one of Napoleon's Imperial Eagle Standards in the early-19th century. The Museum also tells the exciting story of the Armagh, Monaghan and Cavan Militias.

Where is it?
Armagh County Museum
The Mall East
Armagh
Co. Armagh
BT61 9BE

Royal Irish Fusiliers Museum
Sovereign's House
The Mall
Armagh
Co. Armagh
BT61 9DL

Who do I contact?
For information on Armagh County Museum please contact:
Tel: 028 3752 3070
Fax: 028 3752 2631
Email: acm.info@magni.org.uk
Website: www.armaghcountymuseum.org.uk

For information on the Royal Irish Fusiliers Museum please contact:
Tel: 028 3752 2911
Fax: 028 3752 2911
Email: rirfus-museum.freeserve.co.uk
Website: www.rirfus.museum.freeserve.co.uk

What do I need to know?
Armagh County Museum is open from Monday to Saturday between 10.00am and 5.00pm (but closes between 1.00pm and 2.00pm on Saturday). Disabled access and internal lift. Giftshop. Workshops are available at Armagh County Museum for primary school visits and should be

booked with the school visit in advance. The Royal Irish Fusiliers Museum is open on weekdays from 10.00am to 12.30pm and from 1.30pm to 4.00pm. Open on Bank Holidays with the exception of Christmas and New Year's Day.

ARMAGH OBSERVATORY AND PLANETARIUM

Armagh Observatory and Planetarium are two of the best-known features of the city. The Observatory was established in 1790 by Archbishop Richard Robinson, who did so much to develop Armagh as a centre of outstanding Georgian architecture and of learning. The Observatory, which is a modern astronomical research institute with a rich heritage, was part of Robinson's dream to create a University at Armagh, and was meant to provide the basis for a School of Sciences for the new institution. Since its foundation, the Observatory has deservedly gained a world-wide reputation for its scientific achievements, particularly in the field of astrophysics and associated sciences.

The Observatory Grounds and Astropark include scale models of the solar system and the Universe, two sundials and historic telescope domes and other outdoor exhibits. A new facility, the Armagh Human Orrery, is located close to the historic main building of the modern Observatory.

The Planetarium, which is associated with the Observatory, was opened in 1968, and the first Director was Sir Patrick Moore of television fame. The Planetarium is essentially a shop-window for science, and was among the first of its kind in the United Kingdom. Its role is to be pro-active and to reach out to the community.

Just across the road from the Planetarium is the Royal School Armagh, which dates back to 1608. Among its former pupils was the Duke of Wellington, as well as Isaac Corry, Speaker of the Irish Parliament in Dublin, and Lord Castlereagh, the former British Foreign Secretary.

Where is it?
Armagh Observatory
College Hill
Armagh
Co. Armagh
BT61 9DG

Armagh Planetarium
College Hill
Armagh
Co. Armagh
BT61 9DB

Who do I contact?
For information on Armagh Observatory please contact:
Tel: 028 3752 2928
Fax: 028 3752 7174
Email: info@arm.ac.uk
Website: http://star.arm.ac.uk *AND*
        http://climate.arm.ac.uk

For further information on Armagh Planetarium please contact:
Tel: 028 3752 3689
Fax: 028 3752 6187

Email: info@armaghplanet.com
Website: www.armaghplanet.com

What do I need to know?
The Armagh Observatory Grounds and Astropark are open all year round, and tours of the Armagh Observatory can be arranged by appointment. For information on opening times for the Armagh Planetarium it is advisable to visit the website or telephone in advance before travelling. There is limited disabled access to the Observatory, but the Planetarium and the Observatory Grounds and Astropark are wheelchair accessible. The Planetarium has disabled toilets and a giftshop. The Planetarium offers a wide range of educational services. Schools and other groups must book their visit in advance. Discount for groups of 20 or more. Armagh Observatory provides occasional out-of-hours tours for educational groups, which can often be tailored to meet the needs of the group. Such tours much be arranged at an agreed cost in advance.

ARMAGH PALACE STABLES HERITAGE CENTRE

The Palace Stables and Heritage Centre was once part of the extensive estate of the Church of Ireland. It was here within the Palace Demesne that Archbishop Richard Robinson lived in palatial splendour in the 18th century, and his successors less so – until it eventually became the headquarters of the local council.

The exhibition in the Palace Stables Heritage Centre

recreates Georgian Armagh in all its grandeur and squalor. Guides in period costume relate Armagh's colourful history and these 'Living History' tours give visitors access to the School Room, Tack Room, Servant's Tunnel and Coachman's Kitchen and more. The beautiful Primate's Chapel has been restored recently and is regarded as one of the best neo-classical Georgian buildings in Ireland.

There is also a restaurant within the Palace complex, and at the entrance to the Demesne on the left are the distinctive remains of a 13th-century Franciscan Friary, which at that time was the longest in Ireland, and a stopping-place for clerical guests. Not far from the Demesne, towards the centre of Armagh, is the City Hotel, which provides rest and refreshment in a modern setting where today's visitors can reflect on an area with so much history.

Where is it?
Palace Demesne
Armagh
Co. Armagh
BT60 4EL

Who do I contact?
Tel: 028 3752 1801
Fax: 028 3751 0180
Email: stables@armagh.gov.uk
Website: www.visitarmagh.com

What do I need to know?
The grounds and restaurant are open all year round. The Heritage Centre is open weekends only during April, May and September; on Saturday from 10.00am to 5.00pm and on Sunday from 12.00 noon to 5.00pm. From June to August the

Centre is open daily from Monday to Saturday between 10.00am and 5.00pm and on Sunday from 12.00 noon to 5.00pm. The restaurant is also open in the evening, and visitors should telephone for details. A 'Living History' presentation and guided tour is available for schools and youth groups who should book their visit in advance. There are walks, a playground and an Eco Trail in the grounds. Disabled access throughout. Giftshop.

ARMAGH PUBLIC LIBRARY

Armagh Public Library was established by an Act of Parliament in 1773, and was the first public library in Ireland outside Dublin. It was the brainchild of the remarkable Archbishop Richard Robinson, the 18th-century Church of Ireland prelate who developed Armagh as a centre of Georgian splendour.

The Armagh Public Library was restored to its former grandeur in 2001, and contains a number of historical treasures, including a valuable first edition of Dean Jonathan Swift's acclaimed *Gulliver's Travels*. The book is made all the more interesting by Swift's hand-written notes for changes to the next print run.

This elegant Library makes visitors most welcome: a Greek inscription above the entrance reads "The Healing Place of the Soul". On display in the library is a French flag, captured at the Battle of Ballinamuck in 1798, the only foreign flag to be captured in Ireland. The Library's contents are shelved not by theme but by size – the computerised catalogue enables staff to access relevant books from this unusual shelving method. Incidentally the proper title is the Armagh Public Library and not, as it is sometimes called 'The Robinson Library'.

Where is it?
43 Abbey St
Armagh
Co. Armagh
BT61 7DY

Who do I contact?
Tel: 028 3752 3142
Fax: 028 3752 4177
Email: ArmRobLib@aol.com
Website: www.armaghrobinsonlibrary.org

What do I need to know?
The Library is open from Monday to Friday between 10.00am and 4.00pm (closed 1.00pm to 2.00pm). Open other times by arrangement. The Library is closed during Bank Holidays. Photocopying is available for research purposes only. Disabled access, with a loop system, and 2 types of chair for easy use by wheelchair users. There are no disabled accessible toilets. Access to the Library itself is free, but guided tours are available at a small fee, with a reduction in price for groups of 25 or more. Schools and other groups should book their visit and inform Library staff of their areas of interest in advance, as books are sometimes sent off-site for conservation purposes.

CARDINAL O'FIAICH HERITAGE CENTRE

The Cardinal O'Fiaich Heritage Centre was established in memory of one of the best-loved Archbishops of Armagh Cardinal Tomas O'Fiaich, who was also Roman Catholic Primate from 1979-90. He was a native of South Armagh, and had a notable academic career before his elevation to the Primacy. He was also a warm-hearted man, who could relate to all kinds of people. His tomb, together with those of former Archbishops D'Alton and Conway, is one of three in a well-kept park on a hillside adjacent to St Patrick's Roman Catholic Cathedral.

The Cardinal O'Fiaich Heritage Centre is a fitting tribute to this former historian, and fluent Gaelic speaker. There is an exhibition on Cardinal O'Fiaich's life and times, and his areas of interest including local history, music and culture. The attractive modern building houses a significant corpus of material relating to Irish history and the Gaelic language. Songs and poems from South Armagh can be heard here.

Where is it?
Slatequarry Rd
Cullyhanna
Co. Armagh
BT35 0JH

Who do I contact?
Tel: 028 3086 8757
Fax: 028 3086 8352

Email: ofiaichcentre-cullyhanna@yahoo.co.uk
Website: www.ofiaichcentre.co.uk

What do I need to know?
The Centre is open all year from Monday to Friday between 2.00pm and 5.00pm and on Bank Holidays between 10.00am and 6.00pm. Opening at other times can be arranged by appointment. Discounts are available for groups of 10 and over by arrangement. Disabled access. Facilities include a multimedia exhibit and a research library which includes maps of townlands. Schools and other groups should book their visit in advance.

CRAIGAVON CYCLE TRAIL

The Craigavon Cycle Trail of 35 miles through the Borough of Craigavon is suitable for cyclists of all ages and skills. It is part of Route 9 on the National Cycle Network, which has an extensive coverage throughout the United Kingdom. Part of this route coincides with the towpath along the Newry Canal Way. Over 1/3 of the distance of the Craigavon Trail is traffic-free. Some cyclists may wish to cover the full route, but others can dip in and out at will.

The Craigavon Cycle Trail has a wide range of attractions, including canal towpaths, the Old Coach Road south of Portadown, and 180 hectares of Craigavon City Park, which also has the first purpose-built trail for mountainbikes. This is suitable for families with children and will also challenge more experienced riders.

There are other attractions including the Craigavon Watersports Centre. The Craigavon Cycle Trail also takes in the Oxford Island Nature Reserve, and historic villages such as Waringstown and Bleary. There are a number of Tourist Offices along the way, where a comprehensive map and contacts leaflet is available. Cycle hire, equipment and advice can be obtained locally.

Where is it?
Craigavon Tourist Information Centre
Lough Neagh Discovery Centre
Lurgan
Co. Armagh
BT66 6NJ

Who do I contact?
For further information on Craigavon Cycle Trail please contact Craigavon Tourist Information Centre:
Tel: 028 3832 2205
Fax: 028 3834 7438
Email: oxford.island@craigavon.gov.uk
Website: www.oxfordisland.com

For further information on the National Cycle Network please contact Sustrans:
Tel: 028 9043 4569
Fax: 028 9043 4556
Email: belfast@sustrans.org.uk
Website: www.sustrans.org.uk

What do I need to know?

The Craigavon Trail covers 35 miles, 12 of which are traffic free with otherwise light traffic. The starting point for this looped Trail is Oxford Island Discovery Centre, (*see* page 73), but the Trail can be joined at any point along the route. Facilities are available along the route. The National Cycle Network is a comprehensive network of safe and attractive routes throughout the UK. For further information on these routes please visit their website.

DAN WINTER'S HOUSE

Dan Winter's House is one of two important landmarks in the Diamond area of Co. Armagh, near the Richhill-Loughgall area. It is also known as "the birthplace of the Orange Order". The House is a mid-18th century listed building, which was comprehensively restored several years ago. The cottage is the ancestral home of the Winter family from before 1700, and contains original artefacts and relics from the Battle of the Diamond, as well as old farming and dairy implements. The Battle of the Diamond took place on 21 September 1795, between the Protestant 'Peep O'Day Boys' and the Catholic Defenders.

The 'Peep O'Day Boys' were victorious, and later the same evening they met at Dan Winter's house to discuss the forming of the Orange Institution before meeting later that evening at Sloan's House in Loughgall. In the aftermath of the Battle of the Diamond, the Royal Black Preceptory was formed in 1797.

Where is it?
9 Derryloughan Road
The Diamond
Loughgall
Co. Armagh
BT61 8PH

Who do I contact?
Tel: 028 3885 1344
Email: winter@orangenet.org
Website: www.orangenet.org/winter

What do I need to know?
The house is open April to September from Monday to Saturday between 10.30am and 8.30pm and on Sunday between 2.00pm and 8.30pm. Open October to March from Monday to Saturday between 10.30am and 5.30pm and on Sunday from 2.00pm to 5.30pm. Closed on Christmas Day and Boxing Day. Disabled access. Giftshop. An educational room is available for schools and other groups who should book their visit in advance. Catering is available for group visits if pre-booked. There is no admittance charge, but visitors are asked to give a donation towards the house's upkeep.

DERRYMORE HOUSE

Derrymore House is a National Trust property situated on the outskirts of Bessbrook, near Newry. It is a handsome late-18th century thatched house built by Isaac Corry, who was Speaker in the old 18th Irish Parliament in Dublin. He represented Newry in that Parliament for some 30 years from 1776, and the historic 1800 Act of Union between Britain and Ireland was signed in Derrymore House. There is a Treaty Room tour which underlines the significance of this event. Other National Trust properties in the area include Ardress House at Annaghmore near Portadown, and The Argory at the Moy.

Derrymore House is adjacent to the 'Model Village' of Bessbrook, which was founded in 1845 by the philanthropist Quaker John Grubb Richardson, who established a linen mill in the village. It was based broadly on a William Penn settlement in the USA, and Bessbrook inspired the Cadbury family in their development of the Bournville garden township, near Birmingham.

Bessbrook was established without police, pawnshops and public houses, and although police were introduced in 1897 (against the Richardson family's wishes) the village is still without a pawnshop or pubs. The nearby villages, however, have plenty of public houses! Visitors to Bessbrook can still see the distinctive lines of the village, and there is access available to one of the former mill cottages in College Square.

Where is it?
Derrymore House
Bessbrook
Newry
Co. Armagh
BT35 7EF

Who do I contact?
Tel: 028 8778 4753 (The Argory)
Fax: 028 8778 9598
Email: derrymore@nationaltrust.org.uk
Website: www.ntni.org.uk

What do I need to know?
The grounds are open daily from May-September from 10.00am to 7.00pm, and open daily from October-April from 10.00am until 4.00pm. Last admission 30 minutes before closing. Telephone The Argory on 028 8778 4753 for Treaty Room opening times. Disabled access throughout. Group discounts available.

GOSFORD FOREST PARK

Gosford Forest Park covers a large area of woodland and parkland and provides excellent walks and scenery. The Park was originally Gosford Demesne and was home to the Acheson family and their descendants, the Earls of Gosford, for several centuries. They established woodland, parkland and other features which visitors can still see today. The way-marked trails in the forest all begin and end in the Wheel car park and routes are clearly sign-posted.

There are various trails and paths which wind through the forest and into the Park's most beautiful and tranquil areas before heading back to their starting point. The Castle Path is around 2km in length and takes in the Arboretum and part of the Walled Garden before it reaches the edges of privately owned Gosford Castle. The path then leads through wood plantations and past the rare breed and heritage poultry enclosures.

The longer Greer's Trail is around 4.2km in length and takes visitors to Dean Swift's Well and Chair. Jonathan Swift, most famous for writing *Gulliver's Travels*, was a family friend of the Achesons and stayed with them. His connection to the area is still celebrated. The trail leads along the Drumlack River to the millponds, once used to store water for the millwheel, but now an ideal environment for flora and fauna who thrive in water. The trail then journeys through beech and coniferous forest plantations. The Crunaght Trail (6.2km) leads on from Greer's Trail back over the Drumlack River to open parkland and the deer and rare breed enclosures.

Where is it?
Gosford Forest Park
Markethill
Co. Armagh
BT60 1GD

Who do I contact?
Tel: 028 3755 1277
Website: www.forestserviceni.gov.uk

What do I need to know?
Gosford Forest Park is open all year, every day from 8.00am to sunset. Amenities and activities offered in the Park include camping and caravan sites, picnic and barbecue areas, walking trails, orienteering and horse

riding. Telephone the Head Forester on 028 3755 2169 to book recreational facilities from Monday to Friday between 10.00am and 12.00 noon. Schools and other groups can book guided tours through the Head Forester before their visit. Disabled access. Special events can be arranged by permit.

LOUGHGALL COUNTRY PARK

Loughgall Country Park is set in a large beautiful estate of orchards, open farmland and gardens, with an attractive lake. It provides a wide range of activities for people of all ages – including walking, golfing, fishing and riding. There is also a children's play area and adventure trail, and a shop and refreshment area.

There is an Orchard Walk of 3km and a Lakeside Walk of 2km, which provide excellent trails through beautiful woodland and countryside. There are picnic tables and seating at various parts of the Country Park, and car parking is available for a small fee.

The attractive 18-hole Golf Course is set in mature woodlands, and there are daily rates as well as annual subscriptions available. There is also a golf-shop on site. The 37-acre Coarse Fishery is well stocked, and a licence is required before a daily or yearly permit can be bought. Dead bait and small consumable items can be purchased for fishing. There is also a Bridle Path of 6km through woodland and open countryside, which is available for exercising horses or ponies for a daily or yearly rate. A horsebox park is also available.

Where is it?
11-14 Main Street
Loughgall
Co. Armagh
BT61 8HZ

Who do I contact?
Tel: 028 3889 2900
Fax: 028 3889 2902
Email: g.ferson@btinternet.com
Website: www.visitarmagh.com

What do I need to know?
Loughgall Country Park is open daily year-round from Monday to Friday between 9.00am and dusk, and on Saturday and Sunday between 7.30am and dusk. Disabled access. The Park has walks, a Trim Trail and children's play and adventure areas. Sporting opportunities include a football pitch and an 18-hole golf course, which is available at a group discount to golf societies. Caravan clubs can pre-book the arena area during summer weekends. The Park does not have a restaurant, but there is a coffee bar facility.

MAGHERY COUNTRY PARK AND LOUGH NEAGH

The Maghery Country and Caravan Park provides good

access to Lough Neagh, and there is also a play area, picnic tables and a caravan park. Situated at Maghery village, only 5 miles from the M1 motorway, it provides an area of calm in a busy world. The Park covers some 30 acres, with woodland parks and facilities for fishing, birdwatching and walking.

There are several local walks and trails around the southwestern shore of the Lough, with its rich wildlife and natural habitats. There are three longer routes – the Orange, Black and Blue routes – of varying distances, ranging from 5 to 12 miles. These link the Maghery Country Park and the nearby Peatlands Park to the broad area of the River Blackwater, the River Bann and Lough Neagh. Restaurants, cafés and toilets are available along the way.

Coney Island is the only inhabited island in Lough Neagh, and it lies 1km offshore from the Country Park. The island has a rich history which traditionally goes back to St Patrick, and is said to have been one of the most westerly outposts of the Norman conquest in the North. Visitors can take boat trips out to Coney Island from the jetty at Maghery Country Park.

Lough Neagh is popular with the boating fraternity and Kinnego Marina is the largest marina on the lough. It has 140 berths and is a Royal Yachting Association training centre. Training is offered in Powerboating, Sailing, Personal Water Craft, Sea Survival and VHF marine radio by fully qualified instructors. But boat trips on Lough Neagh are available on board the *Master McGra* for those who simply want to sit back and relax.

Where is it?
Maghery Country Park is on the southwestern shore of Lough

Neagh. Take Exit 12 from M1, 8 miles east of Dungannon.

Who do I contact?
For further information on Maghery Country Park, please contact the Events Team at Lough Neagh Discovery Centre:
Tel: 028 3832 2205
Fax: 028 3832 2205
Email: oxford.island@craigavon.gov.uk
Website: www.oxfordisland.com

For further information on Kinnego Marina and boat trips to Coney Island please contact:
Tel: 028 3832 7573
Email: Kinnego.marina@craigavon.gov.uk

What do I need to know?
Maghery Country Park is open from April to the end of September from Monday to Saturday between 10.00am and 6.00pm, and on Sunday from 10.00am to 7.00pm. From October to the end of March, the Park is open daily from 10.00am to 5.00pm. Disabled access. Giftshop. The Park offers conference facilities, and can cater for educational groups – there are guides available – which should be booked in advance. Kinnego Marina is situated in Oxford Island National Nature Reserve and offers boating services and amenities including training in maritime techniques by fully qualified instructors. Camping and caravan sites with all the necessary amenities are available but must be pre-booked. Please contact Kinnego Marina for further information on all boat trips.

The Navan Centre is situated almost two miles west of Armagh, just off the main Caledon-Killylea Road. It tells the gripping history of early Ulster when Navan was the seat of the Kings of Ulster. Exhibits at the Navan Centre let visitors tour the 'Vanished World' of lost myths, explore the 'Real World' of archaeology, then enter the 'Other World' to listen to the Ulster Cycle legends. After this preparation, you are ready to walk the path of history to the great ancient Seat of Kings, Navan Fort.

At Navan Fort – the ancient site of Emain Macha from which Armagh derives its name – archaeologists have found evidence of the existence of a huge temple in Celtic times. The name 'Navan' is itself a derivation of the ancient name of this settlement, *Emain Macha*, which was mentioned by Ptolemy in the second century AD, and was known to be a flourishing centre at the time of Christ.

During the ascendancy of the Ulster Kings, this area was the centre of the political, social and religious life of the Province. It has been described as the Irish equivalent of King Arthur's Camelot, the base for the Knights of the Round Table. It is highly likely that St Patrick established his first main church in Armagh because of its secular and ecclesiastical power-base. The Navan Centre is an important stopping point for those who wish to know more about the history of this extremely important area.

Where is it?
Navan Centre
81 Killylea Road
Armagh
Co. Armagh
BT60 4LD

Who do I contact?
Tel: 028 3752 1801
Fax: 028 3751 0180
Email: navan@armagh.gov.uk
Website: www.visitarmagh.com

What do I need to know?
The grounds are open all year. The Navan Centre is open during April, May and September at weekends – on Saturday from 10.00am to 5.00pm and on Sunday from 12.00 noon to 5.00pm. The Centre is open daily from June to the end of August from Monday to Saturday between 10.00am and 5.00pm and on Sunday from 12.00 noon to 5.00pm. Other times by arrangement for tour groups or educational visits. Closed on 12th July. Disabled access to most areas (the top of the fort is not accessible to wheelchair users). An Education Officer is available for school and youth groups, who should book their visit in advance. An audiovisual presentation is available in French, German, Irish, Italian and Spanish. Guided tours are available for a fee and visitors should telephone for details of times and group discounts. A giftshop and baby changing facilities are also available at the Centre. For information on forthcoming events please visit the website or see local press for details.

OXFORD ISLAND AND LOUGH NEAGH DISCOVERY CENTRE

Lough Neagh is the largest freshwater lake in the British Isles. It is also a region of major environmental importance, with a number of areas now classified as National Nature Reserves.

Oxford Island is located on the shores of Lough Neagh close to the Lurgan turnoff of the M1. Owned and managed by Craigavon Borough Council, it was designed as a Nature Reserve due to its wide variety of habitats, such as reedbeds, open water, wildlife ponds and wildflower meadows. The reserve covers an area of 282 acres and has five bird watching hides as well as four miles of footpaths. The children's play area combines a paddling pool, a water play feature and lots of other play equipment at the Lough Neagh Discovery Centre, adds another dimension to the variety of facilities available to visitors at Oxford Island.

Lough Neagh Discovery Centre, opened in 1993, is the starting point for any visit to Oxford Island or Lough Neagh. With its superb setting on the shores of Lough Neagh and environmental events the Centre is an excellent destination for day trips, family days out, wildlife enthusiasts and group visits. Staff at the Centre have expert knowledge of the reserve and local wildlife to help visitors make the most of their visit. A programme of events is held throughout the year at the Centre to cater for anyone interested in wildlife and the countryside. This ranges from themed walks to talks on subjects such as birdwatching, wildflowers or woodlands, to practical conservation activities such as tree planting and countryside access events.

Where is it?
Lough Neagh Discovery Centre
Oxford Island National Nature Reserve
Lurgan
Co. Armagh
BT66 6NJ

Who do I contact?
Tel: 028 3832 2205
Fax: 028 3831 1699
Email: oxford.island@craigavon.gov.uk
Website: www.oxfordisland.com

What do I need to know?
The Centre is open from April to September from Monday to Saturday between 10.00am and 6.00pm, and on Sunday from 10.00am to 7.00pm. Winter opening hours run from October to March when the Centre is open daily between 10.00am to 5.00pm. Giftshop. An education programme is available for students from primary school age up to university level. Schools and other groups should book their visit in advance. The Centre can also cater for other groups who wish to avail of walks and other activities on request. Maps and easy to follow self guided trail guides are available from reception. The Centre has an information office for details on local tourist attractions and meeting rooms can be pre-booked for conferences or other events. For information on forthcoming events please visit the website or see local press for further details.

ARMAGH

Slieve Gullion Forest Park in South Armagh, near Newry, is an area of outstanding beauty, and a 10km drive through this mountainous park offers excellent views of the surrounding countryside. The area is steeped in legend and history and it is traditionally associated with Cúchulainn and the Red Branch, and also the giant Finn McCool. In the 17th century this was the haunt of Redmond O'Hanlon, a local brigand said to resemble Robin Hood, who allegedly robbed the rich to give to the poor.

The mountain drive has its own delights, but for those with an eye for history, there is also a walk to the top of Slieve Gullion, with its ancient passage grave, and a cairn and volcanic lake. According to legend those who venture into the lake will find their hair turning grey!

For the less energetic, there is a scenic, gentle 2km walk through a mature woodland, and an excellent walled garden. There is a coffee shop at the Courtyard Centre. This listed building holds exhibitions and craft workshops: it is also a conference facility and a heritage education centre. There are other interesting sites around the area, including Killevy Old Church, and a drive to Forkhill and Crossmaglen provides a wide range of interest and scenery. To the north is the lovely Camlough Lake and the nearby 'Model Village' of Bessbrook, as well as the historic National Trust property Derrymore House (*see* page 62).

Where is it?
89 Drumintee Road
Killevy
Co. Armagh

Who do I contact?
Tel: 028 3084 8084
Fax: 028 3084 8028
Email: forestservice@dardni.gov.uk
Website: www.forestservice.gov.uk

What do I need to know?
Slieve Gullion Forest Park is open from Easter to the end of September all week between 10.00am and dusk. Disabled access. Giftshop. Other facilities include picnic areas and information maps. Schools and other groups should book the education centre in advance. For information on forthcoming events please visit the website or see local press for details.

ST PATRICK'S CHURCH OF IRELAND CATHEDRAL

St Patrick's Church of Ireland Cathedral stands on the hill known as *Druim Saileach* (Sallow Ridge) where, according to tradition, Ireland's patron saint founded his first main church in 445 AD. A notice board outside the Cathedral confirms this pre-eminent site in Irish ecclesiastical history. Inside there is a long list of Abbots, Bishops and Archbishops of Armagh from Patrick's time to the present day. On the outer wall on the north side there is a large plaque to the memory of the former High King of Ireland Brian Boru. He died at Clontarf in 1014 in the last great battle to repel the Vikings from Ireland and was buried at the Cathedral.

There were many changes to the cathedral down the turbulent centuries of warfare and pillage, as well as natural destruction and fire. Accordingly the church was rebuilt at least 17 times, and the present elegant structure dates from the last major restoration in 1834. William Makepeace Thackeray described the interior as "neat and trim like a lady's drawing-room". The Cathedral was again refurbished beautifully in recent years.

There are important memorials to those who helped shape the history of the Church and of the country, including Lord Rokeby the 18th-century Archbishop who created the Georgian splendour of Armagh city, and founded the Robinson Library and the Observatory. In the Cathedral there is an Iron Age statue of a small figure known as 'the Tandragee man'. Also on display is a broken cross, dating from the 11th century. The outstanding stained-glass includes an unusual depiction of Patrick in a toga – emphasising his Roman origin – and also a more traditional portrait, as a Biblical figure laying the foundation stone of his first main church.

Where is it?
Cathedral Close
Armagh
Co. Armagh
BT61 7EE

Who do I contact?
Tel: 028 3752 3142
Fax: 028 3752 4177
Email: ArmRobLib@aol.com
Website: www.stpatricks-cathedral.org

What do I need to know?
The Cathedral is open daily from April to October between 10.00am and 5.00pm, and November to March between 10.00am and 4.00pm. Disabled access. There is a discount for groups of over 25 people, on both guided and non-guided tours. Groups must book their visit and tour in advance. Telephone for details of tour dates and times.

ST PATRICK'S ROMAN CATHOLIC CATHEDRAL

This particularly beautiful Cathedral sits on a hill directly opposite its Protestant counterpart, and on a site where traditionally St Patrick had carried a fawn on his shoulders to a "safe place", with its doe following.

The Cathedral was the early-19th century vision of Archbishop Crolly who had bought the site from the Earl of Dartrey. The construction began on St Patrick's Day in 1840, but building was interrupted for several years during the Irish Famine, when funds were used to feed the sick and hungry. The 'Famine line' in the brickwork of the walls, marking the beginning of further construction can still be seen today. There were many delays, and although the exterior was completed in 1873, the interior was not finished until 1904, when the Cathedral was consecrated. During the construction, there were many fund-raising drives, including a Grand Bazaar in 1865. A large grandfather clock still remains in the Vestry as an unclaimed prize.

The Cathedral has several impressive stained-glass windows, including a magnificent portrait of Patrick as a Bishop who is baptising two Irish princesses. High above are pictures of both the Protestant and Catholic Cathedrals, which are grouped together in an ecumenical gesture long before the term had been invented. The Cathedral, which was magnificently refurbished recently, is light and airy with a mixed architectural elegance and colourful history, as depicted by the slowly decaying red hats of former Cardinal Archbishops of Armagh.

Where is it?
Cathedral Road
Armagh
Co. Armagh
BT61 8BE

Who do I contact?
Tel: 028 3752 2638
Fax: 028 3752 2638
Email: armaghparish@btconnect.com
Website: www.armaghdiocese.org

What do I need to know?
The Cathedral is open to visitors daily all year. Open during May to August between 9.00am and 8.00pm, and from September to April daily between 9.00am and

6.00pm. The giftshop is open Monday to Friday between 10.30am and 12.30pm, 3.00pm and 5.00pm, Saturday between 10.30am and 12.30pm, 8.00pm and 8.30pm. On Sunday the giftshop is open between 12.00 noon and 1.00pm, 3.00pm and 5.00pm. Disabled access and toilets. Giftshop. Entry to the Cathedral is free, but there is a charge for guided tours. Contact directly for details of tours and discounts for schools and other group visits which must be booked in advance. When enquiring about guided tours, give details of areas of interest and the tour can be adapted to suit.

ST PATRICK'S TRIAN

St Patrick's Trian is an excellent exhibition centre and complex in Armagh which relates the history of Armagh and of St Patrick himself. The name 'Trian' originates from the division of the old city into districts, called 'trians'.

The complex has three major exhibitions, each with an Armagh connection. The 'Armagh Story' follows the city's pagan monuments from their origins, through the arrival of Celtic Christianity and on to the modern city. The 'Patrick's Testament' display, vividly portrays the story of Patrick and his times from the writings found in *The Book of Armagh*. The 'Land of Lilliput' exhibition, where *Gulliver's Travels* by Dean Jonathan Swift is narrated by a 20-foot tall giant. As a young man, Swift had connections with the Armagh area.

The Trian also has a gift-shop, with souvenirs of Armagh and a wide range of books and literature on Armagh and St Patrick. There is also a restaurant, stylish craft shops and a tourist information centre. The complex is used for conferences, art exhibitions and other events. Individuals and tour groups are welcome, and the Trian is also an important educational centre for children and young people.

Where is it?
40 English Street
Armagh
Co. Armagh
BT61 7BA

Who do I contact?
Tel: 028 3752 1801
Fax: 028 3751 0180
Email: info@saintpatrickstrian.com
Website: www.visitarmagh.com

What do I need to know?
The Trian is open year round from Monday to Saturday between 10.00am and 5.00pm, and on Sunday from 2.00pm to 5.00pm. Closed during 12th July and Christmas holidays. Disabled toilet facilities and access throughout. Giftshop. Facilities are available for conferences and other events. Educational facilities are available for schools and other groups who should book their visit in advance. Tour guides are available on request and touch screen technology is available in French and German. For information on forthcoming events at St Patrick's Trian please visit the website or see local press for details.

The Tannaghmore Gardens and Farm Museum is located near the Craigavon Lakes, and provides contact with a wide range of farm animals, including a number of breeds which are rare or close to extinction. These include Irish Moiled cattle, one of the rarest in the world; Dexter cattle, one of the smallest; and Galway sheep which are one of the rarest breeds in the British Isles. There are saddleback pigs – known in Ireland as 'The Beltie' – as well as geese, hens, turkeys, ducks, pheasants, guinea fowl and peafowl, and also rabbits.

There is also a listed Georgian farmhouse with a beautiful rose-garden, and picnic and barbecue areas, as well as a children's play area. There is a Barn Museum, which displays farming activities in Co. Armagh from past times. The Animal Farm and Museum specialise in tours for schools and other groups, and visitors can help with the feeding of lambs, kids and poultry. It is also possible to synchronise tours in advance with the anticipated hatching of chicks.

Where is it?
Tannaghmore Gardens and Farm Museum
Silverwood
Kilvergan Road
Craigavon
Co. Armagh
BT66 6LF

Who do I contact?

Tel: 028 3834 2115
Fax: 028 3834 3244

What do I need to know?

The Farm is open year-round from 10.00am until 1 hour before dusk. The Barn Museum is open on Sunday between 11.30am and 6.00pm from April to September. Winter opening hours can vary and it is advisable to check before travelling. Disabled access to most areas. Contact the Educational Team on 028 3832 2205 for details of tours for schools and other groups, which should be booked in advance. There are rare breeds of cattle and poultry on the farm, and the Barn Museum has displays on farming activities. Barbecue facilities available.

TI CHÚLAINN CULTURAL ACTIVITY CENTRE

The Ti Chúlainn Cultural Activity Centre is situated in South Armagh and is dedicated to fostering and developing the Irish language and culture. This new purpose-built centre is situated at Mullaghbawn (Mullach ban) in the Ring of Gullion. It is owned by the local community and was opened in 1998 – though the Ti Chúlainn organisation was established some eight years earlier.

The Centre offers several cultural and language courses at all levels, for local and international visitors. There is an archive with an extensive collection of folklore gathered by Michael J. Murphy and others, and it contains sound, written and photographic material on the cultural heritage of the area. This includes folk and traditional music, English and Gaelic, as well as dance, drama, folklore, literature and archaeology.

The Centre has 15 en-suite bedrooms, a main function hall and audio-visual room and an exhibition area, as well as a residents' lounge and gift shop.

Where is it?
An Mullach Ban
Newry
Co. Armagh
BT35 9TT

Who do I contact?
Tel: 028 3088 8828
Fax: 028 3088 6693
Email: tichulainn@btconnect.com
Website: www.tichulainn.com

What do I need to know?
The Centre is open weekdays from 9.00am to 5.00pm year round. Disabled access. Gift shop. There is an audio-visual room for school and youth groups, who should book their visit in advance. For further information on courses, accommodation or forthcoming events, please contact the Ti Chúlainn Centre directly.

COUNTY DOWN

BALLYCOPELAND WINDMILL

Ballycopeland Windmill, near Millisle, is a prominent feature of the local Co. Down landscape. It is a tall whitewashed tower, built in the late-18th century, and is one of over 100 windmills which were located throughout Co. Down. However, it is thought to be the only working windmill surviving in Ireland today.

This forerunner of modern alternative energy sources through wind-power was in operation until around 1915, when the McGilton family ceased milling, and the structure lay disused for many years. Following extensive renovation by the Environment and Heritage Service of Northern Ireland it was made functional, and began working again in 1978.

However, it is not usually in operation during visiting hours, which are clearly listed on a notice-board outside the building. The milling process is best observed by climbing to the top floor and working downwards. Nearby are the Miller's house, which contains an audio-visual presentation, and the grain-store.

Where is it?
Windmill Road
Millisle
Co. Down

Who do I contact?
Tel: 028 9181 1491
Fax: 028 9182 0695
Website: www.ehsni.gov.uk

What do I need to know?
Open daily during July and August (except for Monday).
Opening hours vary with day and visitors are advised to check
before travelling. As a general guide the Windmill is open
on afternoons between 2.00pm and 6.00pm on Tuesday,
Friday, Saturday and Sunday and in the morning between
10.00am and 1.00pm on Wednesday and Thursday. Very
limited disabled access. Visitors can watch a video of the
milling process and the history of Ballycopeland Windmill.

BANGOR

Bangor is a popular resort with first-class sailing facilities
and superb views over Belfast Lough and the Antrim Coast.
Like other Northern Ireland seaside towns, it was once a
mainly 'bucket-and-spade' resort, but it now boasts a range
of tourist facilities, including an extensive marina which is
one of the best of its kind in the British Isles.

On the far side of the Marina is the Pickie Family Fun Park. Numerous attractions for children include Giant Swan pedal boats, paddling pools, a miniature railway, and adventure playgrounds. There is also a café. Bangor offers bracing coastal walks, attractive beaches and – at the Town Hall – the informative North Down Heritage Centre, as well the historic 6th-century Bangor Abbey, founded by St Comgall during the flowering of early Irish Christianity. The Bangor Hand Bell, made of solid bronze and found in the old Abbey graveyard, can be seen at the Heritage Centre. Collections and archives at the Centre, which has Registered Museum status, include local archaeological and maritime heritage, as well as famous local personalities.

Bangor is easily accessible from Belfast, and the town provides an excellent base for sampling the many other tourist attractions of the area, including Groomsport, Donaghadee, and the charming 18th-century Church of St Andrew at Balligan, on the Dunleath estate.

Where is it?
Bangor Tourist Information Centre
34 Quay Street
Bangor
Co. Down
BT20 5ED

Who do I contact?
Tel. 028 9127 0069
Fax: 028 9127 4466
Email: tic@northdown.gov.uk
Website: www.northdown.gov.uk

For further information on North Down Heritage Centre please contact:
Tel: 028 9127 1200
Email: heritage@northdown.gov.uk
Website: www.northdown.gov.uk/heritage

What do I need to know?
Bangor Tourist Information Centre is open all year. As a general guide opening times are Monday to Friday between 9.00am and 5.00pm, and on Saturday between 10.00am and 4.00pm. From June to August the Centre also opens on Sunday between 1.00pm and 5.00pm. Opening times are extended to 6.00pm from Monday to Friday during July and August. North Down Heritage Centre is open Tuesday to Saturday between 10.30am and 4.30pm, and on Sunday between 2.00pm and 4.30pm. These opening hours extend to 5.30pm in July and August. The Centre opens on Bank Holidays. Disabled access and facilities for partially sighted visitors. Giftshop. An educational tour is available and should be booked in advance. Contact the Education Office on 028 9127 8031 for further details. Although admission is free, a donation helps the Heritage Centre. For information on forthcoming events please visit the websites or see local press for details.

BRONTË HOMELAND INTERPRETATIVE CENTRE

The area between Banbridge and Rathfriland was the paternal home of the famous Brontë sisters and the Brontë Homeland Interpretative Centre at Drumballyroney explains this historic and important connection. Their father Patrick Brunty, the eldest of a family of ten, was born locally on 17th March 1777. Apprenticed to a blacksmith before becoming a weaver, the self-educated Patrick was taken up by the Rev Andrew Harshaw who obtained a teaching post for him at Glascar. He then taught at Drumballyroney before going on to study at St John's College, Cambridge, where he changed his name to Brontë. After graduating he came back to Drumballyroney to preach his first sermon after which he returned to England where he became Rector of Haworth in Yorkshire.

The Brontë Homeland Drive, through attractive countryside, takes in the main features of the family's Northern Irish background. The ten-mile route is well signposted. It begins at Drumballyroney which is near the hilly town of Rathfriland, and some ten miles from Banbridge on the main Belfast-Dublin route. The Brontë Homeland area also provides access to the superb scenery of the Mourne Country.

Where is it?
Church Hill Road
Drumballyroney
Rathfriland
Co. Down
BT34 5PH

Who do I contact?
For further information on the Brontë Homeland Interpretative Centre please contact:
Banbridge Gateway Tourist Information Centre
200 Newry Road
Banbridge
Co. Down
BT32 3NB

Tel: 028 4062 3322
Fax: 028 4062 3114
Email: tic@banbridge.gov.uk
Website: www.banbridge.com

What do I need to know?
The Brontë Homeland Interpretative Centre is open from March to September, from Friday to Sunday between 12.00 noon and 4.30pm. The Centre is open by appointment at other times. Schools and other groups should book their visit in advance. Group discounts available. Giftshop. There are picnic tables in the Centre's grounds. Symbols refer to the Brontë Homeland Interpretative Centre.

CASTLEWELLAN FOREST PARK

Castlewellan Forest Park offers a wide range of activities to visitors, and contains one of the best-known and outstanding shrub and tree collections in Europe. The magnificent National Arboretum was established in the mid-18th century, and greatly developed by the fifth Earl of Annesley from 1870. The land for the Park was leased from the Annesleys in 1967, before its official establishment within the Forest Service two years later.

There is a most impressive range of trees and plants in the arboretum and the beautifully kept gardens. These include the Chinese *Kerria Japonica* 'Pleniflora' and the exotic *Crinandron Hokeranum*, as well as plants from Mexico, the Himalayas and many other parts of the world.

The Park has a mile-long lake, with marked trails around the shores and through the forest. One of the latest attractions is an imaginative Peace Maze, which was established with the help of community volunteers, and one of the great challenges to visitors is to find the elusive Peace Bell at the centre – a perfect symbol for all the politicians as well.

Just behind the Park on the Bannonstown Road is the Mount Pleasant Pony-Trekking and Horse-Riding Centre which, for over 30 years, has catered for novice and experienced riders with many different backgrounds and skills.

Where is it?
Main Street
Castlewellan
Co. Down
BT31 9BU

Who do I contact?
Tel: 028 4377 8664
Fax: 028 4377 1762
Email: customer.forestservice@dardni.gov.uk
Website: www.forestserviceni.gov.uk

What do I need to know?
Open daily from 10.00am until sunset. Some disabled access. An education room is available for schools and other groups who should book their visit in advance. Guided tours are available for schools but must be booked in advance on 028 4377 2252. Other Park facilities, which should be pre-booked, include a caravan site and fishing. The Park also has orienteering routes and picnic areas.

Castle Ward, which is owned by the National Trust, is a unique 18th-century house set in a beautiful 820-acre estate with stunning views across Strangford Lough. Sadly, the first Viscount Bangor, Bernard Ward and his wife Anne could not agree on the style of their new home – or seemingly much else, for they later parted!

However they did compromise on the house. In architecture she favoured Strawberry Hill Gothic, while he preferred Classical – so the house unusually has façades in each style, with *his* at the back and *hers* at the front! This diversity is also reflected in the somewhat claustrophobic and cluttered interior, but it is still well worth a visit.

The extensive grounds at Castle Ward include splendid gardens, excellent walks, and a fascinating and still functioning corn-mill, as well as woodland and loughside trails and horse-paths. There is also Old Castle Ward, Temple Water and the Strangford Lough Wildlife Centre. There is ample parking, and a restaurant and gift shop. There is also a small theatre in one of the buildings where the Castleward Opera regularly stages good-quality productions. The Strangford Ferry, offering easy access to Portaferry on the other side, leaves regularly from a jetty just a short distance away.

Where is it?
Strangford
Downpatrick
Co. Down
BT30 7LS

Who do I contact?
Tel: 028 4488 1204
Fax: 028 4488 1729
Email: castleward@nationaltrust.org.uk
Website: www.ntni.org.uk

What do I need to know?
Grounds open every day from May to September between 10.00am and 8.00pm and from October to April between 10.00am and 4.00pm. Admission to the house is by guided tour. House opening times vary and visitors should check before travelling. As a general guide it is open at weekends from April to June and during September between 1.00pm and 6.00pm. The house is open every day during July and August between 1.00pm and 6.00pm. Last house tour begins at 5.00pm. The cornmill is only operational on Sunday during July and August. The tea room and giftshop are open during house opening hours but close at 5.30pm. Castle Ward has good facilities for school groups (which should be pre-booked) and include an education room and hands-on activities for children to try. Group discounts available. Disabled access to most areas. For information about forthcoming events, please visit the website or see local press for details.

The village of Dundrum, several miles north of Newcastle, lies on the edge of an attractive bay, which provides excellent walks and a rich variety of wildlife and birdlife. There are also the remains of a fine 12th-century Norman castle, which stands on a rock above the inner bay. This was built to guard the major land routes from Drogheda to Downpatrick, and in 1210 it hosted no less a celebrity than King John himself. Admission is free. There are nominated opening times. The excellent Dundrum Bay Walk begins and finishes at the north end of the village, and covers some four miles along public roads and a disused railway track which was once the main line from Belfast to Newcastle.

The coastal section along the former track provides a wide range of interests for botanists and ornithologists, and also for the non-expert visitor who enjoys a bracing walk in beautiful surroundings. Among the many plants of interest are Smith's Cress, wood vetch, and a number of different wild orchids, in season. The Bay Walk brings the visitor back to the village by road, or if preferred, by a return trek along the coastal route.

Dundrum Bay is a major winter refuge for a wide variety of wildfowl, including dunlin and widgeon, as well as sea duck, grebes and shag. To the south lies the famous Murlough Nature Reserve, also with a stunning variety of birdlife, and wildlife. This National Trust reserve includes rabbits, badgers and stoats, as well as rare Dexter cattle and Exmoor ponies introduced to preserve the area's biological diversity.

Murlough covers an extensive area of sand dunes, with heathland and woodland, and some 22 species of butterflies, as well as delicate flowers like the pyramidal orchids and carline thistle. Murlough has one-fifth of all the dune heathland in the British Isles, and its vegetation attracts willow warblers and whitethroats, as well as in winter the fieldfare and redwing, which feed on the orange berries. Another location worth exploring is the nearby Tyrella, which also has remarkable range of sand dunes, and a good beach which provides excellent views of the Mourne region.

Where is it?
South Down Office
Murlough National Nature Reserve
Dundrum
Co. Down
BT33 0NQ

Who do I contact?
Tel: 028 4375 1467
Fax: 028 4375 1467
Email: murlough@nationaltrust.org.uk
Website: www.ntni.org.uk

What do I need to know?
Murlough National Nature Reserve is accessible year-round. An Information Centre and toilets, open throughout the Summer, are located in the car park. A boardwalk suitable for wheelchair users runs from the National Trust car park through the dunes to the beach, which is several miles long. Schools and other groups should book their visit in advance.

Holiday cottages nearby are available to rent throughout the year. Symbols refer to Murlough Nature Reserve.

EXPLORIS AQUARIUM

Exploris at Portaferry near Strangford Lough is Northern Ireland's award-winning aquarium. It provides an important focus for those who want to find out more about marine life of the oceans, the coastal waters and the shorelines.

There is an Open Sea Tank, which affords a close-up view of the wonders of the deep, with its sharks, rays and other sea-life. The Marine Discovery Lab has its own small pool where the displays are changed regularly in a year-long programme of exhibitions and activities for children. Exploris also contains the fascinating Northern Ireland Seal Sanctuary, which gives refuge and a temporary home for orphaned or sick seal pups. These are cared for and re-introduced to their natural habitat at an appropriate stage of their recovery. There are times when no seals are 'in residence', and it is therefore advisable to check for such details in advance.

However, with or without seals, Exploris has much to offer the visitor, and it is one of the major tourist and visitor attractions in Northern Ireland. The Strangford Peninsula itself is also worth exploring, and there is a regular ferry between Portaferry and Strangford, which navigates expertly the sometimes tricky waters of the Lough.

Where is it?
Exploris Aquarium
The Rope Walk
Castle Street
Portaferry
Co. Down
BT22 1NZ

Who do I contact?
Tel: 028 4272 8062
Fax: 028 4272 8396
Email: info@exploris.org.uk
Website: www.exploris.org.uk

What do I need to know?
Opening times vary with time of year and visitors should check before travelling. As a general guide summer opening hours run from April to August when Exploris is open on weekdays from 10.00am to 6.00pm; on Saturday from 11.00am and on Sunday from 12.00 noon to 6.00pm. Winter opening times operate from September to March when Exploris is open on weekdays from 10.00am to 5.00pm, on Saturday from 11.00am to 5.00pm and on Sunday from 1.00pm to 5.00pm. Discounts available for groups of 8 or more, with some reductions for children and disabled visitors. There are guided talks every 90 minutes (with a supervised opportunity to touch some exhibits) and in season there is a 4.00pm talk on the work of the Seal Rescue facility. An Education Suite is available for schools and youth groups who should pre-book their visit. Disabled access throughout. Giftshop. There is a caravan site, bowling green and children's play park next to the aquarium. For further information on forthcoming events please visit the website or see local press for details.

The ruins of the Cistercian Grey Abbey are situated at the neat little village of the same name, on the shores of Strangford Lough. This 12th-century church and cloister is one of the best examples of Anglo-Norman ecclesiastical architecture in Ireland.

The Abbey was founded in 1193 by Affreca, wife of the Earl of Ulster John De Courcy. The early Cistercian monks were self-sufficient in farming and in growing herbs for medicinal purposes to help local people and even animals. Grey Abbey today boasts a replica medieval herb-garden or 'physick garden' with more than 50 varieties of plants. There is also a Visitor Centre, and an exhibition which provides a glimpse of life in Ireland in Norman times.

The Abbey is set in the parkland of the 18th-century Rosemount House. The grounds of the house are private, but visitors are welcome to stroll around the ruins of the Abbey. There is also an historic cemetery nearby. Informal car parking is available, and staff are on-site to provide a history of the ruins, and also general information. The village of Greyabbey is noted for its antique shops.

Where is it?
9-11 Church Street
Greyabbey
Co. Down
BT22 2NQ

Who do I contact?

For further information on tours of Grey Abbey please contact:
Tel: 028 9023 5000

For further information on Grey Abbey please contact the Environmental Heritage Service:
Tel: 028 9054 6754
Fax: 028 9054 6516
Email: ehsinfo@doeni.gov.uk
Website: www.ehsni.gov.uk

What do I need to know?

Grey Abbey is open at weekends from October to March, on Saturday between 10.00am and 4.00pm and on Sunday between 2.00pm and 4.00pm. From April to September the Abbey is closed on Monday, but open from Tuesday to Saturday between 9.00am and 6.00pm, and on Sunday from 1.00pm to 6.00pm. Staff are available on site to provide a history of the Abbey. The Abbey has a Visitor Centre and Exhibition Centre. Schools and other groups should book their visit in advance and guided tours are available (please telephone for details). Children under 16 must be accompanied by an adult. Disabled access and toilet facilities. Picnic area.

HILLSBOROUGH

Hillsborough, south of Lisburn, is an historic centre with buildings of charm and of considerable architectural interest.

There are several good restaurants and shops in the main street, and Hillsborough has the ambience of a prosperous English village – which is not surprising, given its close historic connection with the Crown.

Hillsborough Castle, a late-18th century mansion, is set on a hill in the heart of the village, and was the former seat of the Governors of Northern Ireland. It also has been the official residence of successive Northern Ireland Secretaries of State, as well as the overnight residence of Her Majesty Queen Elizabeth II and other members of the Royal Family during their visits to Northern Ireland. Investitures and other official functions are held in the Castle, and the premises can be booked, with permission, for a selected range of private and charitable functions.

The nearby Courthouse is architecturally distinctive, and has an absorbing exhibition on 'The Law in Ireland'. Hillsborough Fort, across the road, dates from the mid-17th century. It is set in the beautiful Hillsborough Forest Park with its attractive lake, well-marked walks and a rich variety of wildlife and birdlife. Also worth visiting at the bottom of the main street is the beautiful late-18th century Anglican (Church of Ireland) with its elegant tree-lined avenue, and the nearby grave of Sir Hamilton Harty, the distinguished Ulster-born classical musician known as the "Irish Toscanini".

Where is it?
Hillsborough Tourist Information Centre
The Courthouse
The Square
Hillsborough
Co. Down
BT26 6AG

Who do I contact?
For information on visiting Hillsborough please contact:
Tel: 028 9268 9717
Fax: 028 9268 9773
Email: tic.hillsborough@lisburn.gov.uk
Website: www.visitlisburn.com

For information on Hillsborough Courthouse please contact:
Tel: 028 9054 3030

What do I need to know?
The Tourist Information Office in Hillsborough Courthouse is open year-round from Monday to Saturday between 9.00am and 5.00pm, with extended opening hours during Summer. Disabled access. Giftshop. The Courthouse shares these opening hours. Guided tours are available and schools and other groups should book their visit in advance.

KINGDOM OF MOURNE

This extensive region in the southeast is one of the most interesting, scenic and historic areas of Northern Ireland. The Mourne Mountains, with their rugged peaks and poetic names like Slieve Binnian and Wee Binnian, as well as the larger Slieve Martin, Slieve Muck and Slieve Donard (the highest) provide endless delight for the visitor, as well as superb scenery. The Mourne Area of Outstanding Natural Beauty includes the mountains, foothills and the coastline which Percy French celebrated in song.

The Kingdom of Mourne, with its fields enclosed by intricate stone walls, its myths and legends, and its canny people, is virtually a place apart. However it is accessible by relatively good roads, and a good touring map is essential. There are a number of drives (and cycle-rides), and a visit to the Spelga Dam and the Silent Valley Reservoir provides welcome tranquility in a busy world.

The main population centres are Newcastle, Annalong and Kilkeel, capital of the Kingdom of Mourne, where – just outside the town on the road to Rostrevor – there is a charming coffee shop run by the Mourne Grange Camphill Community. A round trip through Rostrevor, Warrenpoint, Hilltown and back to Newcastle provides much variety and scenic beauty. The fascinating Tollymore Forest Park, not far from the town of Newcastle itself, was the first State forest to be designated a Forest Park in 1955. It has many attractions – including historic trees and plants and architectural and natural rarities – and is also well worth visiting for the views it affords of the Mournes and the sea.

Where is it?
The Kingdom of Mourne's historical boundaries run from south of Newcastle (St Patrick's stream) to the Cassy Water east of Rostrevor and inland to include the peaks of the Mournes.

Who do I contact?
For further information on the Kingdom of Mourne please contact Mourne Heritage Trust:
Tel: 028 4372 4059
Fax: 028 4372 6493
Email: mht@mourne.co.uk
Website: www.mournelive.com

What do I need to know?

Mourne Heritage Trust Office, at 87 Central Promenade, Newcastle, is open Monday to Friday from 9.00am to 5.00pm all year. Closed on Public Holidays. Disabled access. Giftshop. There are guided walks and cycle events, as well as lectures of public interest. For information on forthcoming events, please see the website or local press for details.

MOUNT STEWART

Mount Stewart, near Newtownards, is a distinctive 18th-century mansion owned by the National Trust, with outstanding gardens and a rich history. The house has 19th-century additions, and it was the home of the British statesman Lord Castlereagh, who was Foreign Secretary during the Napoleonic Wars.

The house has many remarkable furnishings and historical artefacts, including 22 chairs used at the Congress of Vienna from 1815-16. There is also the distinctive portrait of the racehorse Hambletonian painted by George Stubbs in 1799, and the hooves of Fightin' Charlie, the racehorse which won the Gold Cup with jockey Lester Piggott. One fascinating exhibit is the small porcelain figure of a German trooper presented by Von Ribbentrop, one of Hitler's associates, during a visit to Mount Stewart just before the Second World War.

The Mount Stewart Gardens are exceptional, and have been nominated as a World Heritage Site. The complex includes the Shamrock Garden, the superbly landscaped Sunken Garden, the Spanish Garden and also the Dodo Terrace with its stone ark and dodos. There is a beautiful lakeside walk and also worth noting is the late-18th century Temple of the Winds designed by James 'Athenian' Stuart. This has a spiral staircase and it affords good views over Strangford Lough. Guided tours of the Mount Stewart house are available.

Where is it?
Mount Stewart House
Portaferry Road
Newtownards
Co. Down
BT22 2AD

Who do I contact?
Tel: 028 4278 8387
Email: mountstewart@nationaltrust.org.uk
Website: www.ntni.org.uk

What do I need to know?
Opening hours vary with time of year and visitors should check before travelling. As a general guide the Lakeside Gardens are open daily all year between 10.00am and sunset. Mount Stewart House is generally open at weekends from mid-March to April and during October between 12.00 noon and 6.00pm. Open daily during May (except Tuesday) and June from 1.00pm to 6.00pm. Extended daily opening hours operate from July to September between 12.00 noon and 6.00pm. The Formal Gardens are open daily during April and October between 10.00am and 6.00pm and from May to September between 10.00am and 8.00pm. The House and Formal Gardens are closed from November to February.

Last admission to the House and Formal Gardens is one hour before closing. The Temple of the Winds is open from April to October on Sundays, Bank and Public Holidays between 2.00pm and 5.00pm. Disabled access. Gift shop. An education room is available for schools and other groups who should book their visit in advance. Group discounts are available. For further information on forthcoming events at Mount Stewart please visit the website or see local press for details.

NENDRUM MONASTIC SITE

Nendrum Monastery, traditionally founded in the 5th century by St Machaoi – a follower of St Patrick – is situated on the attractive Mahee Island in Strangford Lough. It is surrounded on three sides by water, but is readily accessible by bridges. The site has an air of quiet, ecclesiastical antiquity, as well as excellent views and an audio-visual exhibition and other displays.

The Monastery was reputed to have provided a wealth of local converts, who helped to form Christian communities in other parts of Ireland, as well as in the British Isles and further afield. There are documentary references to the Monastery from the 7th century, until 976 AD when the Abbot was reportedly burned alive in his House, possibly during one of the many Viking raids in the area. However, the site retained its sacred connections, and a small Benedictine cell was established at Nendrum in the late-12th century. It remained a parish church until 1306, but lay abandoned for many years, after a new church was established during the 15th century at Tullynakill on the mainland.

The Nendrum site remained in ruins for centuries until the distinguished church historian William Reeves re-discovered them in the mid-19th century, during a search for the church recorded in 1306. The ruins were substantially restored, following excavations in the 1920s, and a summer cottage dating from the early-20th century is now a Visitors Centre.

Where is it?
The monastery is found on Mahee Island in Strangford Lough. The island is connected to the mainland by narrow lanes and causeways, and can be found off the A22 just south of Comber. There are no public transport links to the island, and the road is not suitable for large coach traffic.

Who do I contact?
Tel: 028 9181 1491
Fax: 028 9182 0695
Email: ehsinfo@doeni.gov.uk
Website: www.ehsni.gov.uk

What do I need to know?
There is open access to the monastic site at all times. The Visitors Centre is open from October to March on Saturday between 10.00am and 4.00pm and on Sunday between 2.00pm and 4.00pm. From April to September the museum is open from Tuesday to Saturday between 9.00am and 6.00pm and on Sunday between 2.00pm and 6.00pm. Guided tours are available by arrangement for schools and other groups, who should book their visit in advance. Children under 16 years must be accompanied by an adult.

The seaside resort of Newcastle sits at the foot of Slieve Donard. It is a good base for touring the beautiful Mourne area, which is one of the major tourist attractions in Northern Ireland. Slieve Donard, which rises to almost 3,000 feet, is the highest mountain in the Province, and traditionally derives its name from St Domangard – a disciple of St Patrick – who was said to have lived as a hermit in one of the pre-historic burial cairns on the mountain.

Donard is popular with climbers of all skills and of all ages, and detailed information about walking in the Mournes is available from the Tourist Information Centre in Newcastle. However, extreme care should be taken by climbers and trekkers, as the mountainside can be extremely dangerous in inclement weather, or if visitors move off the well-known tracks. In all cases, suitable clothing and footwear should be worn. A good starting point is Donard Park, which has a car park and picnic facilities.

Apart from the scenic attractions, Newcastle and the surrounding area have achieved lasting fame because of Percy French, who composed the haunting emigrant's lament about 'The Mountains of Mourne'. There is a memorial to commemorate the 1910 flight by the Ulster inventor Harry Ferguson in his home-made monoplane.

Where is it?
Newcastle Tourist Information Centre
Newcastle Centre

10-14 Central Promenade
Newcastle
Co. Down
BT33 0AA

Who do I contact?
Tel: 028 4372 2222
Fax: 028 4372 2400
Email: newcastle.tic@downdc.gov.uk
Website: www.downdc.gov.uk

What do I need to know?
Newcastle Tourist Information Centre is open daily year-round. From July to August, the Centre opens from Monday to Saturday between 9.30am and 7.30pm, and Sunday between 1.00pm and 7.00pm. In September, and from April to June, it opens from Monday to Saturday between 10.00am and 5.00pm, and Sunday from 2.00pm to 6.00pm. Sunday opening hours from October to March are between 2.00pm and 5.00pm. The Tourist Information Centre is wheelchair-accessible. Giftshop.

ROWALLANE GARDENS

Rowallane Gardens, near Saintfield, is an outstanding National Trust property which offers magnificent flowering and other displays, including the National Collection of Penstemons. It also houses the Northern Ireland headquarters of the National Trust.

Rowallane has a sense of beauty and timelessness, with acres of quiet beauty and – in season – a remarkable and colourful display of rhododendrons and azaleas. Much of the credit for the early development of Rowallane is due to the Reverend John Moore, who laid it out in the mid-1860s. His nephew, the well-known botanist Hugh Armitage Moore, inherited the property in the early-20th century and spent some five decades creating and improving the gardens.

One of the attractions of Rowallane has been the introduction of many new species of plants and trees from around the world, while retaining the permanent character of the rolling landscape. The rock garden and the walled garden, with their rare plants and flowers, are particularly striking, as are the several wildflower meadows. The estate is attractive all the year round, but particularly so in spring and early summer, as well as in the autumn.

Where is it?
Rowallane Gardens
Saintfield
Ballynahinch
Co. Down
BT24 7LH

Who do I contact?
Tel: 028 9751 0131
Fax: 028 9751 1242
Email: rowallane@nationaltrust.org.uk
Website: www.ntni.org.uk

What do I need to know?
The Gardens are open daily except on 25th-26th December and 1st January. Opening times vary with

time of year but as a general guide are open from April to September between 10.00am and 8.00pm, and from September to April between 10.00am and 4.00pm. Last admission is 30 minutes before closing. There is a tea room and visitors are advised to check opening times. The Gardens are partially accessible to disabled visitors and there are 2 wheelchairs available for visitors on a first-come, first-served basis. Disabled parking and adapted toilet facilities. Guided tours and group visits should be booked in advance. For information on forthcoming events at Rowallane Gardens please visit the website or see local press for details.

SCRABO TOWER AND COUNTRY PARK

Scrabo Tower is a well-known landmark monument on a hillside overlooking Newtownards. It was built in 1857 as a tribute to the third Marquis of Londonderry, for his kindness shown to the local people during the ravages of the earlier Irish famine. It provides stunning views over Strangford Lough and also a broad sweep of North Down, as well as the Mourne Mountains, Belfast and even Scotland, on a good day.

Scrabo Country Park uses the Tower as its centre. The Tower is used to host an introductory display on the Hill and surrounding area. The Tower has two floors with displays, and a climb of 122 steps leads to the open viewing level. The Tower itself is part of Scrabo Country Park, which has a range of scenic woodland walks and open parkland. The nearby Scrabo Golf Course is a test not only of skill but also of stamina.

Scrabo is within an easy driving distance from Belfast, and a visit to the Tower can be complemented by a tour of the magnificent National Trust property of Mount Stewart and Gardens just beyond Newtownards.

Where is it?
Scrabo Country Park
203A Scrabo Road
Newtownards
Co. Down
BT23 4SJ

Who do I contact?
Tel: 028 9181 1491
Fax: 028 9182 0695
Email: ehsinfo@doeni.gov.uk
Website: www.ehsni.gov.uk

What do I need to know?
Scrabo Country Park is open all year, and the Tower is open from Easter to the last week in September, from Saturday to Thursday between 10.30am and 6.00pm. There is a steep climb to the Tower. Arrangements can be made for disabled visitors to view the Tower close up, but there is only pedestrian access to the Tower. Schools and other groups should book their visit in advance. For information on educational programmes please contact the Park Warden.

The Seaforde Gardens, dating from the 17th century, provide a wide range of attractions as well as an exotic Tropical Butterfly House. A walled-garden extending over five acres is divided into two areas. The precise age of the northern section is unknown, but the enclosing wall was recorded on an estate map dating from 1750.

The northern section was originally a kitchen garden, which provided vegetables for the estate house – the ancestral home of the Forde family – and also for the surrounding neighbourhood. This is now a commercial nursery, with many rare trees and shrubs for sale.

The southern half was originally an ornamental flower garden, but later became an overgrown wilderness. It was restored in the 1970s, and it now has an impressive range of flowering plants, including the National Collection of Eucryphia. Among the attractions of this garden are the Mogul Tower, and in the centre a Hornbeam Maze planted in 1975. The Pheasantry in the outer garden contains large conifers and rhododendrons, some over 100 years old.

The Tropical Butterfly House has an impressive range of exotic and free-flying butterflies, as well as parrots, reptiles and insects – all safely behind glass. The Butterfly House and gardens are both worth visiting.

DOWN

Where is it?
Butterfly House
Seaforde Demesne
Newcastle Road
Seaforde
Co. Down
BT30 8DG

Who do I contact?
Tel: 028 4481 1225
Fax: 028 4481 1370
Email: plants@seafordegardens.com
Website: www.seafordegardens.com

What do I need to know?
Seaforde Gardens and Butterfly House is open daily from Easter to September from Monday to Saturday between 10.00am and 5.00pm and on Sunday between 1.00pm and 6.00pm. Winter opening hours may vary and visitors should telephone for details. Reasonable but improving disabled access. Giftshop. For tea room opening hours please contact 028 4481 1138. Admission cost covers entry to the gardens *OR* the butterfly house but a combined ticket is available. Group discount details on request. Schools and other groups should book their visit in advance. Children's playground.

SOMME HERITAGE CENTRE

The Somme Heritage Centre, situated near Newtownards in County Down, provides a comprehensive history of the involvement of soldiers from Ireland, north and south, during one of the major battles of the First World War. The huge loss of life and the large number of wounded also had a major impact on many thousands of families back home.

It tells the heroic story of the involvement of three volunteer Divisions – the 36th (Ulster) from the North, and the 10th and 16th (Irish) from other parts of the island who fought so gallantly against such well-equipped and determined enemy forces from Germany.

The Somme Heritage Centre also provides important information about the background history of the period. This includes the complex build-up to the crisis over Irish Home Rule, as well as the factors which led to such widespread enlistment in British Army. It relates the recruitment and training of the servicemen, and the extreme hardship of life in the trenches.

This is a significant resource for those who want to know more about a crucial period in Irish and British history, and also to appreciate the enormous courage and appalling sacrifice associated with one of the bloodiest battles of the First World War.

Where is it?
Somme Heritage Centre
Whitespots Country Park
233 Bangor Road
Newtownards
Co. Down
BT23 7PH

Who do I contact?

Tel: 028 9182 3202
Fax: 028 9182 3214
Email: sommeassociation@dnet.co.uk
Website: www.irishsoldier.org

What do I need to know?

Opening hours vary with time of year and visitors are advised to check before travelling. As a general guide the Somme Heritage Centre is open from April to June every Monday to Friday between 10.00am and 4.00pm and on Saturday between 12.00 noon and 4.00pm. Closed Sunday. During July and August the Centre is open on weekdays from 10.00am to 5.00pm and at weekends from 12.00 noon until 5.00pm. From September to March the Centre is open from Monday to Thursday between 10.00am and 4.00pm. Admission is by guided tour. Discounts are available for school and group visits, which should be booked in advance. There are 'weapons talks' held for such groups. Disabled access to all areas. Giftshop. For details of forthcoming exhibitions please visit the website or see local press for details.

ST PATRICK CENTRE

The St Patrick Centre in Downpatrick is at the heart of the town and the surrounding countryside, which is so closely associated with the story of Ireland's patron saint.

Traditionally, Patrick is said to have landed near Saul, several miles from Downpatrick, as he embarked on his 5th-century mission to spread Christianity in Ireland. Saul Church, part of the Church of Ireland, stands on the historic site of an original church, and on a hillside nearby there is a huge stone statue depicting the saint.

The St Patrick Centre is an impressive interactive complex, which tells of Patrick's compelling struggles and achievements, with the aid of the latest technology. These are accessible to a wide variety of audiences, ranging from schoolchildren to tourists and many others who wish to find out more about the Ireland's patron saint. One of the exciting features is a large-scale audio-visual display of the aerial features associated with Patrick. There are also good conference facilities, as well as the Saint Patrick Café and a Craft and Gift shop which provides a wide range of literature about St Patrick. The Centre also has an art gallery, and a tourist information centre.

The Down Museum nearby is worth visiting, as is the ancient Church of Ireland Down Cathedral, beside which the traditional site of Patrick's grave is marked by a large granite boulder. Each St Patrick's day a wreath is placed on this spot. The Struell Wells, not far from Downpatrick, are associated with Patrick and are said to have healing properties.

Where is it?
St Patrick Centre
53a Lower Market Street
Downpatrick
Co. Down
BT30 6LZ

Who do I contact?

Tel: 028 4461 9000
Fax: 028 4461 9111
Email: info@saintpatrickcentre.com
Website: www.saintpatrickcentre.com

What do I need to know?

The Centre has varied opening hours depending on the time of year, and visitors are advised to check before travelling. As a general rule, the Centre is open from October to March every Monday to Saturday from 10.00am to 5.00pm, and on Sunday by request only. The Centre is open on St Patrick's Day from 9.30am to 7.00pm. During April, May and September, opening times are Monday to Saturday between 9.30am and 5.30pm and on Sunday between 1.00pm and 5.30pm. June to August opening times are Monday to Saturday between 9.30am and 6.00pm and Sunday from 10.00am to 6.00pm. Disabled access. Giftshop. An Education Room is available for school and youth groups, who should book their visit in advance. Group discounts available. The Centre's facilities include a conference room, art gallery, terrace garden and Tourist Information Centre.

WILDFOWL AND WETLANDS CENTRE, CASTLE ESPIE

The Wildfowl and Wetlands Centre at Castle Espie, near Comber, is a haven for a wide range of wild bird species including Brent Geese, Nene, and Whooper swans. Previously a limestone quarry, with a brickworks, pottery and lime-kiln, and more recently part of a farm, it was opened in

May 1990 by Lady Scott as a Wildfowl and Wetlands Trust Centre.

It offers a tranquil sanctuary, as a part of the Strangford Lough Ramsar site, and for most of the year some 700 wild birds are to be found at Castle Espie. These numbers are increased dramatically each autumn and winter by the influx of migrating birds, and there have been other welcome arrivals, including the birth of the first Black-necked Swan cygnets hatched at the Centre in April 2003.

Castle Espie also has an art gallery, an interpretation room and a gift and coffee shop, as well as providing fascinating walks, and it is an attractive family destination.

Where is it?
78 Ballydrain Road
Comber
Co. Down
BT23 6EA

Who do I contact?
Tel: 028 9187 4146
Fax: 028 9187 3857
Email: castleespie@wwt.org.uk
Website: www.wwt.org.uk

What do I need to know?
Opening times vary with time of year and visitors are advised to check before travelling. As a general guide the Centre is open during November to February on weekdays from 11.00am to 4.00pm (weekends 11.00am to 4.30pm), March to June on weekdays from 10.30am to 5.00pm (weekends 11.00am-5.30pm), July and August on weekdays from

10.30am to 5.30pm (weekends 11.00am to 5.30pm) and September to October on weekdays from 10.30am to 5.00pm (weekends 11.00am to 5.30pm). The Centre overlooks a lake and there is a picnic and children's play area. There is a giftshop and disabled access to most areas. Educational facilities and staff are available on request for school and youth groups and should be booked in advance. Discounts are available for groups of 12 or over. Castle Espie is located on Strangford Lough, 3 miles south of Comber and 13 miles south-east of Belfast. Signposted from the A22 Comber-Killyleagh-Downpatrick Road. For further information on forthcoming events, please visit the website or see local press for details.

BELLEEK POTTERY

The Belleek Pottery is one of the top visitor-attractions in Ireland north and south, and is internationally acclaimed for its production of Belleek Fine Parian China. It was established in 1857, and since then Belleek china has been prized by discerning collectors all over the world.

Each piece is a truly original example of Irish craftsmanship, and any with the slightest flaw are destroyed – in keeping with the practice of one of the original founders John Caldwell, who provided the land required for the building. The first products were made from locally obtained feldspar, which now comes from Scandinavia. Each item is hand-decorated, and requires a high degree of individual skills and artistry.

The Visitor Centre provides a history of the Pottery, and contains several important examples of the craft. These include the Belleek International Centrepiece, which won its fourth gold medal at the Paris Exhibition in 1900. It is believed to have been made in just seven weeks by a Frederick Slater who came to Belleek in 1893. Standing only 28 inches high, and over 16 inches at its widest point, this creation is a hand-made masterpiece. Replicas of the gold medals are displayed with the International Centrepiece in the foyer of the Visitor Centre. This also has a museum, a video theatre and showroom, and a tea room.

Where is it?
Belleek
Co. Fermanagh
BT93 3FY

Who do I contact?
Tel: 028 6865 9300
Fax: 028 6865 8625
Email: visitorcentre@belleek.ie
Website: www.belleek.ie

What do I need to know?
The Pottery is open daily from May to October between 9.00am and 6.00pm. From November to April, opening times change to Monday to Friday from 9.00am to 5.30pm, Saturday from 10.00am to 6.00pm, and Sunday (April only) from 2.00pm to 6.00pm. The Pottery is closed on Sunday from November to March. Disabled access. Giftshop. School and youth groups should book their tours in advance. Group discounts are available by arrangement.

CASTLE ARCHDALE COUNTRY PARK

Castle Archdale Country Park covers more than 230 acres along the shores of Lower Lough Erne, with its main focus at Castle Archdale – some 10 miles northwest of Enniskillen.

It is an area rich in wildlife, with a wide variety of facilities for caravans, pony-trekking, walking, nature trails and fishing and boating. There is a deer enclosure and butterfly garden near the Visitor Centre.

Castle Archdale also has a varied and colourful history, with the courtyard buildings the only remains of a Manor House dating from 1773. On some of the nearby islands, accessible by boat, a number of historical monastic sites were established, and the best known of these include Devenish and White Island. In more recent times Castle Archdale achieved fame as one of the important Allied military bases which played a vital role in the Battle of the Atlantic during the Second World War. Various locations around the Lough were occupied by Allied personnel, and the Belfast-based Sunderland and American Catalina flying-boats were based at Killadeas, and at Castle Archdale itself.

A caravan-park is now situated of the site of the former aircraft hangars, and the important history of this period is told in an exhibition at the Countryside Centre titled 'Castle Archdale at War'. The Centre also has wildlife and geographical displays.

Where is it?
Castle Archdale Country Park
Irvinestown
Co. Fermanagh
BT94 1PP

Who do I contact?
Tel: 028 6862 1588
Fax: 028 6862 1375

Email: ehsinfo@doeni.gov.uk
Website: www.ehsni.gov.uk

What do I need to know?
The Country Park is open daily. Opening hours for the Museum and Visitor Centre vary with the time year and visitors are advised to check before travelling. As a general guide the Centre is open at weekends from Easter on Sunday between 12.00 noon and 6.00pm, and the May Bank Holiday between 11.00am and 6.00pm. From July to August the Museum and Visitor Centre open every day between 11.00am and 7.00pm except Monday. Camping is permitted in the adjacent caravan park. A group campsite is available for groups but must be pre-booked. Pony trekking is available during July and August. There is a family cycle trail. Disabled access. Giftshop. The tearoom is seasonal. Educational programmes are available for nursery age children right up to 'A Level' study groups. Facilities include a classroom, an audio-visual room and WW2 memorabilia. School and other groups should pre-book their visit and discuss their needs with the Educator at the park in advance.

CASTLE COOLE

Castle Coole, situated on the main road north of Enniskillen, is an outstanding National Trust property and one of the best neo-classical houses in the British Isles. It was designed by James Wyatt and completed in 1798, after a decade of building.

Many of the best craftsmen available were involved in the construction and completion of the house, and among the highlights are the State Rooms with their outstanding Regency furnishings. Of particular significance is the magnificent State Bedroom, said to have been prepared for a visit by King George IV in 1821. There is also a beautiful main hall, where concerts are regularly held.

Outside the house, there is much to explore, including a Grand Yard, the former servants' quarters and tunnel, and a restored 'Ice House'. There is also a laundry house and a display room. There are rolling parklands in the 700-acre estate, together with extensive woods and Lough Coole itself. All of this, plus the associated wildlife and birdlife, makes Castle Coole an ideal destination for walkers and for those who enjoy outstanding architecture and fine scenery. The property is licensed for civil weddings.

The other National Trust properties in the area are Florence Court and Crom Demesne.

Where is it?
Castle Coole
Enniskillen
Co. Fermanagh
BT74 6JY

Who do I contact?
Tel: 028 6632 2690
Fax: 028 6632 5665
Email: castlecoole@nationaltrust.org.uk
Website: www.ntni.org.uk

What do I need to know?

Opening hours at Castle Coole vary throughout the year and visitors are advised to check before travelling. As a general guide the Grounds are open daily from April to October between 10.00am and 8.00pm and from November to March from between 10.00am and 4.00pm. The House is open at weekends from 1.00pm to 6.00pm during April, May and September (daily during Easter week). The House is open daily (except for Thursday), during June from 1.00pm to 6.00pm, with extended daily opening during July and August between 12.00 noon and 6.00pm. The House is closed between October and March except for St Patrick's Day. Last admission is one hour before closing. Visits outside normal hours carry an increased cost. Discounts are available to groups, who should book their visit in advance. Tours are available. The House is wheelchair accessible with partial access through the Gardens. Giftshop. Tea room. There are parkland walks where dogs on lead are permitted, a picnic area and outbuildings to view. Castle Coole can be used for functions and further information is available on request.

CROM DEMESNE

Crom Demesne at Newtownbutler on Upper Lough Erne is in the care of the National Trust. It covers nearly 2,000 acres and is one of the most significant freshwater habitats in the British Isles. It also contains the largest surviving oak woodland in Northern Ireland.

Crom Demesne is an important conservation site, and has many varieties of wildlife, including two rare butterflies – the purple hairstreak and the wood white – as well as pine marten and the largest heronry in Ireland. There is a Visitor Centre, with an exhibition, a lecture area and a tea room, as well as a small shop, a slipway, a campsite and seven self-catering cottages. The Centre staff can arrange boat hire and overnight bird- and mammal-watching (for the rare Pine Marten), if required, and a day permit for coarse fishing is also available. There are also facilities for licensed civil weddings.

The 19th-century 'new' Crom Castle is in private ownership, and is not open to the public. Other attractive buildings on the demesne include the Gad Island Tower, known locally as a 'romantic folly', and the ruins of the 17th-century Old Crom Castle, which was destroyed in an accidental fire in 1764 and later abandoned. Other nearby National Trust properties are Castle Coole and Florence Court.

Where is it?
Crom Demesne
Upper Lough Erne
Newtownbutler
Co. Fermanagh
BT92 8AP

Who do I contact?
Tel: 028 6773 8118 (Visitor Centre)
Email: crom@nationaltrust.org.uk
Website: www.ntni.org.uk

What do I need to know?
Opening hours vary, and visitors are advised to check before

travelling. As a general guide the Crom Demesne grounds are open daily from March to September, between 10.00am and 6.00pm (in July to August between 10.00am and 7.00pm). The grounds are open on October weekends only between 12.00 noon and 6.00pm. The grounds are closed between November and March. The Visitor Centre operates at weekends during March and April, and daily from May to September between 10.00am and 6.00pm. Crom Demesne is open on Bank and Public Holidays, including St Patrick's Day. Disabled access. Giftshop. Telephone for details of shop and tea room opening times. Discounts are available for groups who should book their visit in advance. Toilets are available only during Visitor Centre opening hours.

DEVENISH ISLAND

Devenish in Lower Lough Erne is possibly the best-known island in the Lake, and historically it is one of the most important. It was here that St Molaise founded a monastery in the 6th century, along what is thought to have been a regular pilgrimage route to Croagh Patrick. St Molaise's House, a small church building from the 12th century still stands on Devenish.

The site was one of the most important Irish Christian centres of learning, and attracted many students. The marauding Vikings raided Devenish more than once, and as a means of protection against all incursors, a splendid Irish Round Tower was erected on the island in the 12th century. In theory the monks could take refuge high in the 25-metre tower until the raiders had gone, but even holy men could not guarantee their safety at all times!

Modern visitors can still climb the tower, with its excellent views over the remains of an early medieval Christian settlement, and the ruins of the 15th-century St Mary's Augustinian priory, which was abandoned in 1603. There is an unusually intricate cross in the graveyard here. A museum showcases the sculpture from the churches. Apart from its historical resonance, Devenish in fine weather also affords excellent photo opportunities. This rather special "Holy Island" is accessible by ferry from Good Friday until mid-September.

Where is it?
The Ferry to the Island leaves from Trory Point, down a short lane at the junction of B52 to Kesh and A32 to Ballinamallard. 1½ miles from Enniskillen.

Who do I contact?
For further information on Devenish Island please contact the Environmental Heritage Service:
Tel: 028 9054 3037 (Historic Monuments enquiries)
Fax: 028 9054 3111
Email: ehsinfo@doeni.gov.uk
Website: www.ehsni.gov.uk

What do I need to know?
The Museum is open daily from April to September between 10.00am and 6.00pm but in special circumstances visits can be made outside these hours. The site is only accessible by boat (operated by the Environment and Heritage Service), and there is a charge for the ferry, opening the museum and

the toilets. Guided tours of the island are available from the Museum and for further information or to book your visit telephone 028 9054 6518. Schools and other groups should book their visit in advance and for details of the educational programmes on offer please telephone 028 6862 1588. Devenish Island is not suitable for wheelchair users or people with walking difficulties.

ENNISKILLEN CASTLE AND MUSEUMS

Enniskillen Castle dates from the 15th century, when it was the stronghold of the Gaelic Maguire chieftains. It was fought over many times in the local wars. It was captured by the O'Neills and the O'Donnells, and also by the English. The 'new' castle became the focus of a 17th-century Plantation town known as "Inniskilling", and the Castle continued as a troop garrison until the 1950s.

It is now the home of two Museums – the Fermanagh County Museum which features local history and wildlife, and also the Inniskillings Museum which tells the story of the Inniskilling Fusiliers, a regiment formed in 1689. Known as 'the Skins', this was one of the most famous regiments in the British Army, as was a sister regiment the Inniskilling Dragoons. The Duke of Wellington said that the Inniskillings saved the centre of his line at Waterloo, and the defeated Napoleon reflected sadly "That regiment with the castle on their caps – they know not when they are beaten."

Some of the non-military but famous people associated with Enniskillen include the writers Oscar Wilde and Samuel Beckett, who both attended Portora Royal School, as did Henry Francis Lyte who wrote the ageless hymn 'Abide With Me'.

Where is it?
Fermanagh County Museum
Enniskillen Castle
Castle Barracks
Enniskillen
Co. Fermanagh
BT74 7HL

Who do I contact?
Tel: 028 6632 5000
Fax: 028 6632 7342
Email: castle@fermanagh.gov.uk
Website: www.enniskillencastle.co.uk

What do I need to know?
Enniskillen Castle is open all year at varying times and visitors are advised to check. As a general rule, it is open every Monday between 2.00pm and 5.00pm, and Tuesday to Friday from 10.00am to 5.00pm. The Castle is open on Saturday between 2.00pm and 5.00pm except from October to April. The Castle is closed on Sunday except during July and August, when it is open between 2.00pm and 5.00pm. Disabled access and toilets. Giftshop. Fermanagh County Museum has a Learning and Access Officer for school and youth groups, who should book their visit in advance. Educational activity packs are available. There is a discount for groups of 10 or more. Car and coach parking is adjacent to the Castle but not solely for the Museums. For information

on forthcoming events and exhibitions please visit the website or see local press for details.

FLORENCE COURT

Florence Court near Enniskillen is an 18th-century country house in the care of the National Trust, and is one of the most important buildings in Northern Ireland. Situated on a site of sweeping scenic beauty, the Palladian-style building was constructed by Sir John Cole, father of the first Earl of Enniskillen, and romantically named after his wife Florence. It is particularly noted for the rococo plasterwork, which bears the distinctive mark of Robert West of Dublin: this has been beautifully restored by the National Trust. The recent return of significant items from the Earl of Enniskillen's family possessions have added to the distinctive atmosphere of the house.

The furnishings include travelling chests which once belonged to King William III and Queen Mary. There is also a chamber-pot with the features of a former British Prime Minister William Ewart Gladstone inside. (This was one way of recording the local 19th-century opposition to Home Rule for Ireland!)

There is an attractive walled-garden, and the surrounding woodlands contain the progenitor of the world-famous 'Irish Yew' which was discovered by the head gardener in 1767. All Irish Yews are its progeny; as it cannot be truly produced from seed, it has to be propagated from cuttings. The Florence Court Forest Park nearby has a wide variety of habitats, with many mature oaks some two centuries old.

Admission to the house includes a guided tour, and there is also a restaurant. There are extensive walks in the grounds, a saw-mill and a holiday-cottage. Other National Trust properties nearby are Castle Coole and Crom Demesne.

Where is it?
Florence Court
Enniskillen
Co. Fermanagh
BT92 1DB

Who do I contact?
Tel: 028 6634 8249
Fax: 028 6634 8873
Email: florencecourt@nationaltrust.org.uk
Website: www.ntni.org.uk

What do I need to know?
Opening times vary throughout the year and visitors are advised to check before travelling. As a general guide the House is open for guided tours between 1.00pm and 6.00pm on St Patrick's Day, Easter week and at the same hours every Saturday and Sunday during April, May and September. Open daily between 1.00pm and 6.00pm during June (except on Tuesday), and daily from 12.00 noon to 6.00pm during July and August. The tea room and giftshop are available when the House is open. The Grounds are open daily from April to October between 10.00am and 8.00pm and daily from November to March between 10.00am and 4.00pm. There are disabled toilets and access throughout, with Braille and

large-print guides available. Florence Court offers hands-on activities, a children's quiz trail and live interpretation. There is an Education Room suitable for school and youth groups, who should book their visit in advance. Group discounts are available. Groups can also reserve tables in the restaurant. Contact Florence Court for information on special tours and details of country fairs held in the grounds.

LOUGH ERNE

Lough Erne is one of the most beautiful areas of the North, part of a vast waterway which provides boating holidays on two of Ireland's greatest river systems – the Erne and the Shannon. The Erne-Shannon link, opened up recently by the reconstructed Ballinamore-Ballyconnell Canal, enables visitors to explore the many cross-border attractions in both parts of Ireland. The 500-mile waterway traverses a region of superb scenery, with a great variety of wildlife and fishing, and other maritime activities, as well as unique villages, historic buildings and lively entertainment, restaurants and shopping centres.

There are several boat and cruiser-hire companies along the waterway, as well as a multitude of moorings on the islands and shoreline for an overnight stay, or longer. Horse riding and golf are available in several places on the mainland. Upper Lough Erne lies south of the main town Enniskillen and it provides access to the Erne-Shannon Waterway and the heart of central Ireland. The Lough itself has hundreds of islands, many of which are worth exploring, or stopping off for lunch, a picnic, or a little fishing.

Enniskillen itself is a lively town with an early-16th century Castle, good restaurants, pubs and the excellent Ardhowen Theatre, which has an attractive programme of events. Of special interest are the Enniskillen Drama Festival in March, and a Water Sports event in August. To the north of Enniskillen is Lower Lough Erne, stretching as far as Belleek, with its famous Pottery, and also the historic and attractive White Island and its seven ancient Christian stone figures.

Where is it?
Fermanagh Tourist Information Centre
Wellington Road
Enniskillen
Co. Fermanagh
BT74 7EF

Who do I contact?
Tel: 028 6632 3110
Fax: 028 6632 5511
Email: TIC@fermanagh.gov.uk
Website: www.findfermanagh.com

What do I need to know?
For information on cruises on Lough Erne and forthcoming events, contact the Tourist Information Centre. It is open year-round, from Monday to Friday between 9.00am and 5.30pm, with an extension to 7.00pm during July and August. The Centre also opens at weekends from Easter until September when it opens on Saturday between 10.00am and 6.00pm, and on Sunday from 11.00am to 5.00pm. In October opening hours are weekdays from 9.00am to 5.30pm, as well as

Saturday and Sunday between 10.00am and 2.00pm. From November to Easter, the Centre is open on weekdays only. On Bank Holidays the Centre opens between 10.00am and 5.00pm. The Centre is closed Christmas Day and 26th December. Disabled access and help available. Giftshop. There is a 24-hour touch-screen information centre available out of office hours.

LOUGH NAVAR FOREST DRIVE

Lough Navar Forest Drive, some five miles north-west of Derrygonnelly, provides an outstanding panorama over the vast waterway of Lower Lough Erne, and as far away as Donegal Bay in the Irish Republic and the Sperrin Mountains in Northern Ireland.

The seven-mile route, which winds through Lough Navar Forest to the top of Magho Cliffs at a height of 1,000 feet, is well sign-posted. There are ample picnic sites and viewing stops for visitors to look for rare plants and butterflies. There are marked trails, and the visitor may well spot red deer and wild goats.

The Forest Drive leads to the Aghameelan Viewpoint, with the 6km Blackslee Trail, then to the Whiterocks and Lough Slawn Trails (0.5km long), and at Magho Viewpoint there is a vast sweep of rugged and beautiful scenery over the Lough and much further afield. The remainder of the drive leads to 'The Old Man's Head' and Lough Ahork and Trail. Near the exit is the 'Sweat House' which in ancient times was used to alleviate the suffering from rheumatism.

Where is it?
Signposted off A46, Lough Navar Forest is approximately 16 miles from Enniskillen.

Who do I contact?
For further information on Lough Navar Forest please contact the District Forest Office:
Tel: 028 6634 3040
Email: customer.forestserviceni@dardni.gov.uk
Website: www.forestserviceni.gov.uk

What do I need to know?
Lough Navar Forest is open daily year-round between 10.00am and sunset. Consult the Information board at the Park for details. There are picnic sites, trails and walks. Visitors can fish at 3 Department loughs within Lough Navar Forest by permit (available from Home Field and Stream, Enniskillen: telephone 028 6632 2114). Special events can be held at Lough Navar and organisers should contact the Forest Service for information. Toilets are open between Easter and September.

LUSTY BEG AND BOA ISLAND

Lusty Beg island was the 19th-century home of Richard Allingham and this building, known as "Ned's Cottage", has been expertly restored. Later on, Lady Hunt from Canada owned both Lusty Beg and Lusty Mor, but her move to Lusty Beg proved to be most fortunate. Soon afterwards her former residence at Lusty Mor burned down. The remains of the once grand Glenavar House are still visible. The site provides stunning views over the Lough and its islands.

From the mid-20th century, Lusty Beg has been developed successfully as a holiday destination and conference venue. There is a restaurant and other facilities and a local jetty provides access to the nearby islands. At one time Lusty Beg (which means 'fertile and small' in Gaelic) was connected to Lusty Mor (meaning 'fertile and large') by a causeway, and it is still possible to wade across when the water level is low, but due care should be taken.

Boa Island in Lower Lough Erne has an ancient graveyard with two strange figures. The two-faced 'Janus' statue of a Celtic idol would have been of great importance to the Celtic people, who believed that heads retained a special spiritual quality in death. The smaller figure in the old Cladragh burial ground is similar in style. It is thought to have come from another ancient graveyard in the nearby Lusty Mor Island.

Where is it?
Lusty Beg Island
Boa Island
Kesh
Co. Fermanagh
BT93 8AD

Who do I contact?
Tel: 028 6863 3300
Fax: 028 6863 2033

Email: info@lustybegisland.com
Website: www.lustybegisland.com

What do I need to know?
The bar and restaurant on Lusty Beg are open from Easter for the Summer months. Disabled access. Boa Island is reached across a bridge, while Lusty Beg can be accessed by ferry. Activities include off-road driving, archery and a water sports centre. For further information and to book accommodation please contact Lusty Beg directly.

MARBLE ARCH CAVES EUROPEAN GEOPARK

The Marble Arch Caves European Geopark at Florencecourt in Co. Fermanagh is one of Northern Ireland's finest tourist attractions, and affords the visitor access to some of the best show caves in Europe. This is a vast complex of nature's wonders, which were created by the erosion of limestone by rivers and streams draining from the nearby Cuilcagh Mountain.

At Marble Arch Caves, visitors are introduced to a magical underworld of rivers and waterfalls, as well as spacious chambers and winding passages. There are accessible walkways, powered boats moving along a subterranean river, and stalactites and stalagmites to gladden the heart of any curious visitor.

The tour lasts for 75 minutes, and is suitable for people of all ages who are reasonably fit. A sweater and good walking shoes are recommended. Advanced booking for large groups, and at peak times, is advisable. There is good parking, an exhibition area and restaurant, and an audio-visual theatre. Sometimes the caves may be closed due to heavy rainfall, and visitors should check in advance.

Marble Arch Caves and the ruggedly beautiful Cuilcagh Mountain Park are a UNESCO European Geopark, one of only 25 in Europe. The scenic drive along the Marlbank Loop, which provides outstanding views of Lower Lough MacNean, is also worth undertaking.

Where is it?
Marlbank Scenic Loop
Florencecourt
Co. Fermanagh
BT92 1EW

Who do I contact?
Tel: 028 6634 8855
Fax: 028 6634 8928
Email: mac@fermanagh.gov.uk
Website: www.marblearchcaves.net

What do I need to know?
The Marble Arch Caves are open daily from Easter to the end of September. Opening hours from Easter to June and September are between 10.00am and 4.30pm, and during July and August from 10.00am to 5.00pm. Closed from October to just before Easter. There is disabled access to the building but not to the Caves themselves. Giftshop. There is an audiovisual theatre presentation every 20 minutes.

The Caves may be shut if there has been heavy rain, so visitors should check in advance. Schools and other groups should book their visit and tour in advance. There is a discount for groups of 10 or more. Tours run every 20 minutes, with groups of up to 21 people per guide.

WHITE ISLAND

White Island in Lower Lough Erne is the site of an ancient monastery with several remarkable statues of early Christian, or pre-Christian origin. Aligned along the north wall of the ruins, they are thought to pre-date a south-facing Romanesque door. There has been much debate about the origins of the figures, but most scholars agree that they date from the 9th to the 11th century.

Some people believe that the carvings relate to the life of St Patrick, though one grinning 'sheela-na-gig' figure is thought to be a pagan female fertility symbol. Other carvings are thought to represent Christ and King David, and the statue with a crozier is believed to be an image of Patrick himself.

The carvings have survived much history, including the Viking invasions, and almost certainly they pre-date the church itself, which is now a small rectangular ruin, as well as the remarkable Romanesque door. This is thought to date from the late-12th century, as does the church, and the door was restored along with the remains of the church in 1928. It is the only door of this particular antiquity remaining intact in Northern Ireland. White Island, with its ancient mysteries and archaeological gems, can be reached by passenger ferry from Castle Archdale Country Park.

Where is it?
Castle Archdale Country Park
Irvinestown
Co. Fermanagh
BT94 1PP

Who do I contact?
Tel: 028 6862 1588
Fax: 028 6862 1375
Email: ehsinfo@doeni.gov.uk
Website: www.ehsni.gov.uk

What do I need to know?
The ferry service from Castle Archdale Marina operates from April to September. It runs daily during July and August, and at weekends and Bank Holidays during April, May and June. A booking system is available for weekdays during this period. There is a charge for the crossing and each trip lasts one hour. For further information on ferry crossings and to make bookings please contact 028 6862 1333. There are no facilities at the island but a giftshop, toilets and parking are available at Castle Archdale Marina with tea rooms available at Castle Archdale Courtyard.

COUNTY LONDONDERRY

BANAGHER GLEN

Banagher, near Dungiven, is set in an area of great natural beauty and is an important historical centre. Banagher Church – traditionally thought to have been founded by a local saint, Muiredagh O'Heney, dates from the early-12th century, and is now an impressive ruin.

The saint's tomb is located nearby, and according to local tradition, any sand gathered from this place could bring the recipient good luck. However some of the gravestones, including one with a skull and crossbones motif, are a reminder of the limits of mortality.

The Church is set in the beautiful Banagher Glen, some three miles south of Dungiven, which provides outstanding views and challenging walks to the Altnaheglish Reservoir and Banagher Dam. This is also an important area for birdwatching and for investigating flora and fauna.

Near Dungiven, there is also the magnificent Glenshane Pass, on the main road from Derry to Belfast. Watch out for 'The Ponderosa', the highest pub in Ireland, which has a reputation extending far beyond its remarkable location.

Where is it?
For more information on the Banagher Glen area please contact:
Limavady Tourist Information Centre
7 Connell Street
Limavady
Co. Londonderry
BT49 0HA

Who do I contact?
Tel: 028 7776 0307
Fax: 028 7772 2010
Email: tourism@limavady.gov.uk
Website: www.limavady.gov.uk

What do I need to know?
Banagher Glen is open daily all year for pedestrian access. The car park is open at weekends in May, June and September, and daily in July and August. Limited disabled access. The road to the dam is steep. Toilets are available beside the car park. Facilities include an interpretive information board and picnic areas. Symbols refer to Banagher Glen.

BELLAGHY BAWN

Bellaghy Bawn was built as protection for a 17th-century Plantation village. Settlers from England, Scotland and elsewhere were given land in Ulster after the defeat of the Gaelic Irish. However, it was attacked and partially damaged in the rebellion of 1641. Half of the Bawn, consisting of one tower and one house, collapsed in the mid-1700s. The remaining house was then renovated and considerably enlarged by then-owner Bishop Hervey, Earl of Bristol, who also put a new roof on the remaining tower.

The Bawn is now an internationally acclaimed Visitor Centre, which focuses on the work of the Nobel Laureate and poet Seamus Heaney, who comes from the Bellaghy area. The centre contains original manuscripts and other important aspects of his work, including an archive of broadcast and film material. Bellaghy itself is richly represented in Seamus Heaney's work, and students at the Bawn have ready access to important local sites, which provided inspiration for such works as 'The Forge' and 'In Bellaghy Graveyard'. Seamus Heaney, a graduate and former member of staff at Queen's University, was awarded the Nobel Prize for Literature in 1995.

The Bawn was opened to the public in 1996. In addition to the Heaney material, there are exhibitions on the history of the Ulster Plantation, as well as natural and local history. Other plantation sites include Derry's Walls, Dungiven Priory, Roughan Castle, Brackfield Bawn and Draperstown.

Where is it?
Bellaghy Bawn
Castle Street
Bellaghy
Co. Londonderry
BT45 8LA

Who do I contact?
Tel: 028 7938 6812
Email: ehsinfo@doeni.gov.uk
Website: www.ehsni.gov.uk

What do I need to know?

The Bawn is open throughout the year including public and Bank Holidays, but closed Christmas and New Year week. From September to Easter the Bawn is open Monday to Saturday between 9.00am and 5.00pm, closed on Sunday. From Easter to the end of August the house is open daily between 10.00am and 6.00pm. There is limited wheelchair access, but disabled toilets are available. Giftshop. Schools and other groups should book their visit in advance. There is a discount for groups of 10 or more. Bellaghy Bawn has an audiovisual room and a picnic area.

CITY OF DERRY

Londonderry, also called Derry, is one of the best examples of a walled city in Europe, and it has a unique atmosphere where the past retains a huge influence on the present. Derry's Walls, rising in parts to some 30 feet, were built between 1614-18 to protect the new Plantation settlement from the Irish marauders. They successfully withstood sieges in 1641 and 1649, as well as the Great Siege of 1689, during which the Jacobite forces of King James were stoutly resisted by the supporters of King William of Orange. After much hardship the siege finally ended amid much rejoicing and today the Apprentice Boys of Derry still regularly commemorate this victory. Incidentally Derry is also known as the "Maiden City" after surviving so many sieges.

The magnificent Walls were closed during the Troubles, for security reasons, but guided tours are now available. There is much else to explore in Derry, including the Tower Museum and the impressive Church of Ireland Cathedral of St Columb's. This was completed in 1633 in the "Planter's Gothic" style, and was the first Protestant Cathedral to be built in the British Isles after the Reformation. Ironically, it was named after the Irish St Columba who founded *Doire* – 'a place of oaks' – in the sixth century. St Columb's contains many relics of the 17th-century siege, and there is a memorial window to Mrs Cecil Frances Alexander, the wife of a former Bishop of Derry. Her best-known hymns include 'There is a Green Hill Far Away' and 'Once in Royal David's City'.

Across the city is St Eugene's Roman Catholic Cathedral, dating from 1873 and situated near the Bogside with its famous Troubles mural "You Are Now Entering Free Derry". St Eugene's, like its Protestant counterpart, is built on a hill, and it is an elegant building with magnificent stained glass. Another impressive structure is the neo-Gothic Guildhall, set in a Square of the same name, and named in honour of the London Guilds. An earlier building was destroyed by fire in 1908, and its successor was badly damaged during the Troubles. However, it has been magnificently restored, and it symbolises the spirit of a city and its people who have survived much, and continue to flourish.

Where is it?
Derry Visitor and Convention Bureau
44 Foyle Street
Derry
Co. Londonderry
BT48 6AT

Who do I contact?

Tel: 028 7137 7577 OR 028 7126 7284
Fax: 028 7137 7992
Email: info@derryvisitor.com
Website: www.derryvisitor.com

What do I need to know?

Derry Visitor and Convention Bureau is open all year from Monday to Friday between 9.00am and 5.00pm, with Saturday opening from March to June and October between 10.00am and 5.00pm. From July to September opening hours are Monday to Friday between 9.00am and 7.00pm, Saturday between 10.00am and 6.00pm and Sunday opening between 10.00am and 5.00pm. The Centre has disabled access and there is a giftshop and Bureau de Change. Visitors can obtain information on attractions in the area and pre-book accommodation throughout Ireland and the UK. Guided walking tours are available and there is a 24-hour information kiosk. Parking, restaurants and toilets are available in the city centre.

COLERAINE

Coleraine is a lively centre with good shopping, and has been called "this most English of towns in Ulster." Not surprisingly, therefore, its modern foundation dates from the 17th-century Plantation, and in St Patrick's Church, a part of the transept and nave survive from the first settlement of 1613.

Coleraine is associated with St Patrick himself who is traditionally said to have visited "Dunboo...in the barony of Coleraine and the County of Derry" – although it is not clear whether Patrick himself, or a follower, visited the area. However there is much more historical authenticity about Mountsandel on a hill above the River Bann. The large mound, rising to 200 feet, is thought to be the oldest inhabited area in Ireland, and dates back some 9,000 years. There is a well-kept pathway around the mound, and excellent walks along the river. In this broad area of the Bann, archaeologists discovered the 9th-century Dalriada Brooch, and the second-century Bann Disc.

Coleraine is popular with shoppers who like the mix of high-street names and independent family-run shops. The town has numerous cafés and restaurants and the town centre is pedestrianised. A popular attraction for gardeners is the Guy Wilson Daffodil Garden near the local campus of the University of Ulster. Named after an internationally acclaimed breeder of daffodils, it has a unique collection of 400 Irish-bred varieties, and provides a magnificent spectacle at the height of the daffodil season.

Where is it?
Coleraine Tourist Information Centre
Railway Road
Coleraine
Co. Londonderry
BT52 1PE

Who do I contact?
Tel: 028 7034 4723
Fax: 028 7035 1756
Email: colerainetic@btconnect.com
Website: www.colerainebc.gov.uk

What do I need to know?

Coleraine Tourist Information Centre is open from Monday to Saturday between 9.00am and 5.00pm. The Centre has disabled access and there is a giftshop and Bureau de Change. Visitors can obtain information on attractions in the area and pre-book accommodation throughout Ireland. For further information on local events please visit the website or see local press for details.

DOWNHILL DEMESNE AND MUSSENDEN TEMPLE

Downhill Demesne and Mussenden Temple is an extensive National Trust property between Coleraine and Castlerock, which provides outstanding walks and superb views over the Atlantic Coast and Downhill Strand. It was the late-18th century creation of Frederick Augustus Hervey, the wealthy 4th Earl of Bristol, who was also the Church of Ireland Bishop of Derry. The Mussenden Temple, perched on the edge of the cliff-top, was built as a library and was modelled on the Temples of Vesta in Italy. Because of its unique setting, it has long been known as "The Temple of the Winds", and has recently been licensed for weddings.

It was dedicated to the Bishop's cousin, the beautiful Mrs Mussenden, although she died before it was completed. The Bishop was an early champion of Roman Catholic rights, and he made the basement of the Temple available for worship. He was also delightfully eccentric, and it is said that he organised a horse race between Presbyterian and

Anglican clergy on a nearby beach. There was reportedly no gambling on the outcome!

The so-called Bishop's Glen which provides access from the main road to the Mussenden Temple offers a range of attractive landscaped walks and outstanding coastal views. It also leads to the once-magnificent Bishop's Palace, which was rebuilt after a major fire in 1851. The building was inhabited until just before the Second World War, but now lies in ruins. The Lion Gate, beside the remains of a walled-garden, is also of interest.

Where is it?
107 Sea Road
Castlerock
Co. Londonderry
BT51 4TW

Who do I contact?
Tel: 028 2073 1582 or 028 2073 2972 (*North Coast Office*)
Email: downhillcastle@nationaltrust.org.uk
Website: www.ntni.org.uk

What do I need to know?
The grounds are open from dawn to dusk daily. The Temple is open every day during July and August from 11.00am until 5.00pm. Open at weekends during May, June and September from 11.00am until 5.00pm. Also open Bank Holiday Mondays and other public holidays during this period. Dogs on leads only. Good disabled access throughout, but some visitors may require assistance from their companion.

Hezlett House, on the outskirts of Castlerock, is an outstanding late-17th century thatched house, which was a former rectory built for a Church of Ireland Archdeacon of Derry. In 1761 it changed ownership (and religious denominations too!) when it was sold to Isaac Hezlett, a Presbyterian farmer. Not surprisingly, the name was changed to 'Hezlett House', and the family lived there for more than two centuries.

The house, which is easily accessible from the main road leading to Castlerock, is furnished in a simple late-Victorian style. It has a distinctive cruck-truss roof construction, and is one of the very few buildings in Northern Ireland to have survived from its time.

The property has been well maintained by the National Trust, and guided tours are available. There is also a small museum of farm implements. Other areas of interest nearby include Downhill Estate and Mussenden Temple, while the village Castlerock itself has a clean, safe beach and an excellent golf-course.

Where is it?
107 Sea Road
Castlerock
Coleraine
Co. Londonderry
BT51 4TW

Who do I contact?
Tel: 028 2073 1582 OR 028 2073 2972
Email: hezletthouse@nationaltrust.org.uk
Website: www.ntni.org.uk

What do I need to know?
Open during July and August from Wednesday to Sunday.
Open between 12.00 noon until 5.00pm. Guided tour on
admission with last entrance 30 minutes before closing.
Hezlett House is also open on Bank Holiday Mondays during
July and August. Amenities on-site include a picnic area and
baby-changing facilities. Disabled access. Dogs are allowed
on leads and only in garden. School and youth group visits
must be booked in advance. Contact directly for group
discount details.

PORTSTEWART STRAND

Portstewart is a popular holiday resort, with a long and
magnificent beach, excellent walks, and superb views of the
North Coast and of Donegal. The town has much to offer the
visitor. One of its main claims to international fame is that
it was the setting for Jimmy Kennedy's song 'Red Sails In
The Sunset' which describes beautifully a lingering sunset
over the Atlantic Ocean to Donegal, and beyond. The long
promenade has a wide variety of shops, which are becoming
more up-market every year, and there are a number of cafés
where those with time can enjoy food and ice creams as
they watch the world go by. At the end of the promenade

there is a picturesque harbour, where fresh fish are on sale in summer and boating and fishing trips can be arranged.

Leading from the promenade is a beautiful cliff-walk, requiring a little care, but with outstanding views of Donegal and the magnificent Portstewart Strand. This is owned by the National Trust and provides the bracing challenge of a walk to the Barmouth and the River Bann, and back again. The beach is open to motorists but care should be taken with the tides to avoid being trapped in soft sand.

Portstewart has three golf-courses and it is the focal point for the famed North West 200 motorcycle race which is one of the fastest road-races in the world. The race (which also takes in Coleraine and Portrush) is usually held in May and spectators come from all over Ireland and further afield to enjoy the action. Portstewart is prized by all those who appreciate relative quietness and beauty, and it provides a good base for visiting the many tourist and other attractions of the area.

Where is it?
Tourist Information Desk
c/o Portstewart Library
The Crescent
Portstewart
Co. Londonderry
BT55 7AB

Who do I contact?
For further information on Portstewart please contact:
Tel: 028 7083 2286 (July and August)
Tel: 028 7034 4723 (Other times)

Fax: 028 7035 1756
Email: colerainetic@btconnect.com
Website: www.colerainebc.gov.uk

*For further information on Portstewart Strand please contact
the National Trust:*
Tel and Fax: 028 7083 6396
Email: portstewart@nationaltrust.org.uk
Website: www.ntni.org.uk

What do I need to know?
Information is provided at Portstewart Library during July
and August from Monday to Saturday between 10.00am
and 4.30pm, closing for lunch from 1.00pm to 2.00pm. The
Strand and beach are accessible year-round with parking at
Strand Road although admission is charged for access to
Portstewart Strand daily from April to September between
10.00am and 5.00pm, when beach facilities (including
parking and toilets) are available. Symbols refer to Strand.

ROE VALLEY COUNTRY PARK

The Roe Valley Country Park, near Limavady, offers
outstanding scenery, riverside walks, and varied recreational
facilities – and all in an historical context. It extends for some
three miles along the River Roe, with spectacular gorges,
woodland and many kinds of plants and wildlife.

This includes some 60 species of birds, good salmon and trout fishing, and a wide range of riverbank plants and wildflowers. The Country Park also offers many opportunities for canoeing, rock-climbing, orienteering and other challenging outdoor pursuits, as well as a Bio-diversity Trail along flower-meadows and grain fields and past a pond, which provide access for the disabled.

There is also a restored late-19th century hydro-electric power station, a Green Lane Museum which relates the local textile and agricultural history of the area and beyond. There are picnic sites. The Country Park provides many individual and family attractions in an area of beauty and tranquillity.

Where is it?
Roe Valley Country Park
Dogleap Road
Limavady
Co. Londonderry
BT49 9NN

Who do I contact?
Tel: 028 7772 2074
Fax: 028 7776 6571
Email: roevalley2@doeni.gov.uk
Website: www.ehsni.gov.uk

What do I need to know?
The Country Park is open from dawn to dusk. Disabled access to designated trails. An Education Officer is available for schools and youth groups, who should book their visit in advance on 028 7776 7532.

Springhill, owned by the National Trust, is a 17th-century Plantation House at Moneymore and was the home of generations of the Lennox-Conyngham family. It is one of the most charming houses in Northern Ireland, and it has an outstanding library as well as portraits, a nursery, period family furniture, a gun room, and even a ghost called Olivia, the widow of George Lennox-Conyngham. He died by his own hand in 1816 and it is said that his grief-stricken wife has haunted the house ever since.

In the former laundry house there is a remarkable Costume Collection, with some splendid exhibits dating from the 18th-20th centuries, and this is one of the finest features of Springhill. However, there is much else to attract the visitor, including beautiful walled-gardens and a beech tree walk, as well as other marked trails and picnic areas. There is also an Adventure Trail Play Park for children. A visit to the historic Wellbrook Beetling Mill near Cookstown, which is maintained by the National Trust, will fascinate people of all ages.

'Living History' tours at Springhill are available most Sundays from May to August. There is a caravan site, and a barn for hire. There are special events and family days, and also education programmes for primary and secondary school groups.

Where is it?
20 Springhill Road
Moneymore
Co. Londonderry
BT45 7NQ

Who do I contact?
Tel: 028 8674 8210 or 028 8674 7927 (Costume Collection)
Email: springhill@nationaltrust.org.uk
Website: www.ntni.org.uk

What do I need to know?
Open weekends only from April to June from 1.00pm to 6.00pm, except during Easter holiday, when the House is open throughout the week from 1.00pm to 6.00pm. The House is open throughout the week during July and August between 1.00pm and 6.00pm and at weekends during September between 1.00pm and 6.00pm. Guided tour on admission with last entrance one hour before closing. Disabled access. An education room and hands-on activities are available for school and youth group visits (which must be booked in advance). The facilities also include a tea room and a shop. Dogs are only allowed in the garden but must be on leads. There are adult study days, as well as children's quizzes and trails. Contact directly for group discount details.

COUNTY TYRONE

DRUM MANOR FOREST PARK

Drum Manor Forest Park is situated to the south of the Sperrin Mountains and west of Lough Neagh. The estate was formerly owned by a Mr Archibald Close. It was acquired by the Forestry Service in 1964 and opened to the public as a Forest Park in 1970. Since then many of its original features have been enhanced.

Drum Manor is one of a number of well-maintained forest parks in Northern Ireland, and although it is one of the smallest, it has a number of special attractions. These include Japanese and butterfly gardens, an arboretum and parkland. There are also lakes and nature trails.

Drum Manor is worth a visit, in association with a number of other attractions in the area, and it provides a quiet natural focus in the midst of varied and attractive forest scenery.

Where is it?
Drum Road
Cookstown
Co. Tyrone
BT80 8QS

Who do I contact?

Tel: 028 8775 9311
Email: john.millmore@dardni.gov.uk
Website: www.forestserviceni.gov.uk

What do I need to know?

Drum Manor Forest Park is open daily all year round between 10.00am and sunset. Disabled access. There is an information map of the Park's facilities and attractions. The tea room on site is open daily (weather permitting), during July and August. A caravan site offers visitors the opportunity to stay in this Forest Park. Bookings should be made in advance on 028 8676 2774.

GORTIN GLEN FOREST PARK

The Gortin Glen Forest Park, six miles from Omagh, was opened in 1967, and was the first of its kind to be established in purely coniferous woodland. It has many attractions, and one of its main features is a five-mile forest drive, with spectacular views. There are also a number of stops, where the motorist can linger and enjoy the scenery.

The Forest Park is divided into zones, offering walks, biking, and horse-riding. There are three well-marked routes – the Nature Trail, the Pollan Trail and Lady's View Walk – and all trails begin and end in the car park.

These provide visitors with an opportunity to enjoy the flora and the fauna at close range, and they can be modified to suit walkers of all ages and abilities including school and youth groups. There are also three mountain-bike trails which are variously suitable for bikers with basic and moderate skills, while the 'Off-Road' trail is for experienced cyclists only.

Where is it?
163 Glenpark Road
Omagh
Co. Tyrone
BT79 7AU

Who do I contact?
Tel: 028 8167 0666
Fax: 028 8167 9563
Email: stewart.mackie@dardni.gov.uk
Website: www.forestserviceni.gov.uk

What do I need to know?
Gortin Glen Forest Park is open daily between 10.00am and dusk. Walks are colour coded to show ease of access for all visitors. Horse riding is available by permit which should be arranged in advance. Other facilities include picnic and barbecue areas and a camping site. Wedding photographs can be taken by prior arrangement. Guided tours and a classroom are available for schools and other groups but must be booked in advance.

The Grant Ancestral Home is the restored farmhouse where John Simpson, the maternal great-grandfather of the 18th US President Ulysses Simpson Grant, was born. Grant, a distinguished soldier who commanded the victorious Union Army in the American Civil War, later turned to politics. He served for two terms as President from 1869-77, and a year after he relinquished office he returned to his Ulster roots, as part of a world tour.

John Simpson, who was born in 1738, lived at the farmhouse at Derganagh, near Ballygawley. He helped with the hard work of trying to make a living from the land before (at the age of 22) emigrating to America. The ancestral cottage has two rooms with mud floors, and the building and adjacent farmyard have been restored to their mid-19th century appearance.

There is an American Civil War exhibit and an agricultural implements display, as well as audio-visual presentations and a wildlife garden. There is also a tea room and children's play area.

Where is it?
45 Dergenagh Road
Dungannon
Co. Tyrone
BT70 1TW

Who do I contact?
Tel: 028 8776 7259
Fax: 028 8776 0908
Email: killymaddy@dctbc.org
Website: www.dungannon.gov.uk

What do I need to know?
Open March-May and October from Monday to Friday from 10.30am until 4.40pm. Open June-September on Monday to Saturday from 10.00am until 6.30pm and on Sunday from 2.00pm until 6.00pm. Last admissions are one hour before closing.

GRAY'S PRINTING PRESS

Gray's Printing Press in Strabane is cared for by the National Trust. This is where John Dunlap, the printer of the American Declaration of Independence in 1776, learned his trade. Strabane was an important 18th-century printing centre.

Dunlap started his own newspaper – the *Pennsylvania Packet* – which later became America's first daily newspaper. After printing the Declaration of Independence, Dunlap carried the news in his own paper. It is believed that the first daily outside America to print the story was the *Belfast News Letter*. This meant Ulster people probably read the news before King George III himself could do so. Seven of the 56 signatories of the Declaration were of Scots-Irish stock.

James Wilson also learned his trade at Gray's, and emigrated to America five years before Dunlap died in 1812. He married a Sion Mills woman whom he had met on the immigrant ship, and later became a newspaper editor himself in Pennsylvania. Their grandson Woodrow Wilson was the US President from 1913-21, and the ancestral home at Dergalt is open to the public.

The front of Gray's has remained unchanged, and inside there is an exhibition of 19th-century hand-printing machines and an audio-visual presentation, *The Power of Print*. There are occasional demonstrations by a professional compositor. The former shop is now a Museum run by Strabane District Council, and there is also a garden.

Where is it?
49 Main Street
Strabane
Co. Tyrone
BT82 8AU

Who do I contact?
Tel: 028 7188 0055
Website: www.ntni.org.uk

What do I need to know?
Admission to Gray's Printing Press is by guided tour. Open during April, May and September on Saturday between 2.00pm and 5.00pm. Open during June from Tuesday to Saturday from 2.00pm to 5.00pm. From July to the end of August, the Press is open from Tuesday to Saturday between 11.00am and 5.00pm. Gray's Printing Press is closed from October to the end of March. The Printing Press features live interpretation and an audiovisual display. Gray's is level, and

partially accessible to disabled visitors. There is an adapted disabled toilet. Giftshop. Schools and other groups should book their tour in advance. Discounts are available for group visits if booked outside normal visiting hours. Last admission is 45 minutes before closing. For further information about Gray's Printing Press from October to May, please contact Springhill House on 028 8674 8210.

PEATLANDS PARK

The Peatlands Park near Dungannon was officially opened in 1990, and was the first establishment of its kind in the British Isles to promote the importance and awareness of peatlands, and associated issues. There are impressive areas of woodland and bog-land, as well as several small lakes, a nature reserve and walking trails. In the Visitors Centre there is also an exhibition on peat ecology. The many attractions of the Park also include specially created paths, which provide access to the extensive flora and fauna. For transport enthusiasts, there is also a narrow gauge railway.

The Park has two National Nature Reserves, notable for several species not found elsewhere in Northern Ireland. The Annagarriff, or 'Rough Bog' reserve, is particularly noted for its trees, and is the only known site in Ireland for wood ants. The birdlife includes sparrowhawks, jays, long-eared owls and various kinds of warblers, as well as peregrine falcons and hen harriers.

Another reserve within the Park is Mullenakill, or 'Church on the Hill'. This is an 8,000-year-old raised bog sustained by rainfall, which supports a large range of specialised plants, including the Sphagnum mosses. Insects are plentiful, and the occasional lizard is visible, as are snipe and woodcock.

Where is it?
Peatlands Country Park
33 Derryhubbert Road
Dungannon
Co. Tyrone
BT71 6NW

Who do I contact?
Tel: 028 3885 1102
Fax: 028 3885 1821
Website: www.ehsni.org.uk

What do I need to know?
Peatlands Park is open daily from 9.00am to 5.00pm year-round, with extended opening hours from Easter to September. Visitors should make contact for details. School and youth groups should contact the Park for details of the Education Centre when booking their visit. The Park has picnic areas, a souvenir shop and free themed events on Summer weekends. For further information on forthcoming events please visit the website or see local press for details.

The Sperrin Mountains derive their name from the Gaelic term *na Speirini* (meaning 'Spurs of Rock'). This area of outstanding natural beauty lies to the west of the Province, with much to offer the visitor. It stretches from the west of Lough Neagh to Donegal, and contains a myriad of rivers, forests, lakes and shaded glens.

The area includes most of Tyrone, and the southern part of County Londonderry, and stretches almost to the city of Derry itself. The Sperrins have a series of unique valleys – including the Glenelly, Owenkillew, Derg, Roe, Bann and Foyle Valleys – and a wide range of towns and villages, with their own individual characteristics.

The Sperrins remain unspoiled, and offer a wide variety of outdoor pursuits, including equestrian sports, fishing and golf. It is also an area with many scenic drives, though care should be taken when negotiating the narrower and more winding roads. There is also a tremendous variety of walks, with varying challenges and scenic delights.

In the foothills of the Sperrins is An Creagan Visitors Centre, situated at Creggan, on the main road between Omagh and Cookstown. An Creagan's interpretive exhibition provides information about the rich archaeological history of the area, including the Creggandevesky Court Tomb. The Centre's craft shop offers finest quality, hand crafted gifts produced by local craft networks. Trails from the An Creagan Centre take visitors along Glashagh Burn and back to the Centre, a Biodiversity Trail concentrates on the area's raised bogland, and a Storybook Trail, with story panels leads children through local traditional tales and the Sperrin countryside. Archaeological, cultural and environmental tours of the area are also available.

Where is it?
Omagh Tourist Information Centre
1 Market Street
Omagh
Co. Tyrone
BT78 1EE

Who do I contact?
For further information on the area please contact Omagh Tourist Information Centre:
Tel: 028 8224 7831
Fax: 028 8224 0774
Email: omaghtic@btconnect.com
Website: www.omagh.gov.uk

For further information on An Creagan Visitors Centre please contact:
Tel: 028 8076 1112
Fax: 028 8076 1116
Email: info@an-creagan.com
Website: www.an-creagan.com

What do I need to know?
Omagh Tourist Information Centre is open year-round, from October to March from Monday to Friday between 9.00am and 5.00pm, from April to June and September, Monday to Saturday between 9.00am and

5.00pm. In July and August opening hours are Monday to Saturday between 9.00am and 5.30pm. Visitors can obtain information on attractions in the area and pre-book accommodation throughout Ireland and the UK. Giftshop. Exhibition space. An Creagan Visitors Centre offers walking routes, a wheelchair trail and a programme of cultural events for people young and old, with the services of an Education Officer. The craft shop is open Monday to Friday from 11.00am to 5.30pm, Saturday and Sunday from 12.00 noon to 5.00pm. The Centre has a restaurant and bar, conference and function facilities, eight self-catering holiday cottages and a children's play area. Please contact directly for opening times.

TYRONE CRYSTAL

The Tyrone Crystal Centre is an attraction for visitors who want to know more about the art of making crystal. The skill was first brought to Tyrone by Bristol craftsmen in the late-18th century, and they helped to establish the tradition locally. In 1971 this was revived by the enterprising Father Austin Eustace, a local priest who sought to bring employment to the area. Since then, Tyrone Crystal has gained a worldwide reputation for the range and quality of its distinctive hand-made products.

Tours are organised from the Visitors Centre, and experienced guides will bring visitors through the various and fascinating stages of the blowing, marking, cutting and finishing of this special crystal. There is also an opportunity to try some personal glass-cutting, but pre-booking is necessary.

Where is it?
Tyrone Crystal
Killybrackey
Coalisland Road
Dungannon
Co. Tyrone
BT71 6TT

Who do I contact?
Tel: 028 8772 5335
Fax: 028 8772 6260
Email: info@tyronecrystal.com
Website: www.tyronecrystal.com

What do I need to know?
Tyrone Crystal is open year-round from Monday to Saturday, between 9.00am and 5.00pm, and from Easter to Christmas also on Sunday between 1.00pm and 5.00pm. Disabled access. Facilities at the Visitors Centre include an audio-visual suite and a restaurant, and there is also a factory shop with a large collection of crystal and other gifts. Senior citizens, children and groups of 15 or over are admitted free of charge. Tyrone Crystal offers educational tours, with educational packs available on request. Schools and other groups should book their visit in advance.

The Ulster-American Folk Park is one of the outstanding visitor and educational attractions in Northern Ireland. This fascinating open-air museum presents as 'living history' the story of the significant emigration from Ulster to America in the 18th and 19th centuries.

Visitors are taken on a journey following the emigrants from the thatched cottages of the Old World, across the Atlantic to the log cabins of the New World. The outdoor museum, with over 30 authentically furnished exhibit buildings, brings to life people's daily routines and activities in both the Old and New Worlds. Costumed interpreters in traditional Irish thatched buildings and American log houses relate tales of everyday life and customs while demonstrating traditional crafts and skills such as spinning, basket making, printing, quilting, blacksmithing, open-hearth cookery and traditional corn craft.

An Ulster Street with original shop fronts and an American Street have been reconstructed alongside a full-scale dockside gallery and ship. These recreate the conditions that many thousands of emigrants experienced before, during and after the arduous Atlantic crossing. The indoor exhibition 'Emigrants' examines life in Ulster in the 18th and 19th centuries, reveals the reasons behind the exodus and shows how the emigrants adapted to, and impacted on, their new homelands.

Highlights of the Park's activities include spectacular American Independence Celebrations in July, the award winning annual Appalachian and Bluegrass Music Festival, and the ever popular Hallowe'en Festival. A visit to the Museum is a must for anyone who wishes to find out more about the important and continuing link between Northern Ireland and North America.

Where is it?
Castletown
Mellon Road
Omagh
Co. Tyrone
BT78 5QY

Who do I contact?
Tel: 028 8224 3292
Fax: 028 8224 2241
Website: www.folkpark.com

What do I need to know?
The Park is open from April to September every Monday to Saturday between 10.30am and 6.00pm. Open on Sunday and Public Holidays between 11.00am and 6.30pm. Winter opening hours run from October to March when the Park is open from Monday to Friday between 10.30am and 4.30pm. Closed at weekends. Last admission is 1½ hours before closing. Disabled access to most areas. Giftshop. Group discounts on request. Facilities are available for school and youth groups who should book their visit in advance. A wide variety of educational programmes are provided throughout the year for pupils of all ages. These include traditional craft workshops, role-play sessions, dance workshops and a variety of study tours. The Centre for Migration Studies

offers teaching and research support. Visitors are welcome to access the research library and the Irish Emigration Database as part of their visit to the museum. For further details on all aspects of the Park and forthcoming events please visit the website or see local press for details.

CITY OF BELFAST

BELFAST CASTLE

Belfast Castle is a striking building in the Scottish Baronial style. It was erected in 1870 and presented to the citizens of Belfast in 1934 by the Earl of Shaftesbury – whose name is perpetuated elsewhere in the city by a major traffic junction and at least one restaurant and group medical practice. The Castle was built in 1867 and designed by Charles Lanyon.

The Castle is open to the public and it is now a popular venue for weddings and a wide range of other functions. It has a restaurant, and the interior of the building affords sweeping views over the city – including the large shipyard complex stretching out at the mouth of the River Lagan. There is also a good view of the Cavehill Mountain and MacArt's Fort.

The Castle is centred in a spacious and wooded park, with a variety of walks ranging from the leisurely to the challenging – which give a good reason for taking refreshments in the restaurant afterwards. The Castle gardens are attractively laid out, and they are said to be particularly 'animal friendly' with not one but two cat-themed gardens, following a good relationship which was established between the gardeners and a local cat for many years.

Belfast Castle and its grounds provide an attractive venue for a family outing, and lower down the slopes in the shadow of the Cavehill is the children's playground. There is also limited parking near the Castle itself. The Castle has an antiques shop and a Visitor's Centre which relates the history of the building and the Cave Hill. There is even a remote-controlled camera for visitors to admire the views over Belfast Lough and the city itself.

Where is it?
Belfast Castle
Antrim Road
Belfast BT15 5GR

Who do I contact?
Tel: 028 9077 6925
Fax: 028 9037 0228
Email: bcr@belfastcastle.co.uk
Website: www.belfastcastle.co.uk

What do I need to know?
The Cave Hill Antique shop is situated within the castle and is open from Monday to Saturday from 1.00pm-10.00pm and on Sundays from 12.00 noon-5.00pm. The Visitor's Centre is open from Monday to Saturday from 9.00am-10.00pm and on Sundays from 9.00am-6.00pm. Free admission. The Cellar Restaurant is open from Monday from Saturdays for lunches from 12.00 noon to 3.00pm, early evening meals from 5.00pm-6.45pm and dinner from 7.00pm-9.00pm. Snacks and light refreshments are available from 11.00am-5.00pm. Restaurant closed on Monday evenings. The restaurant is open on Sunday for snacks and light refreshments from 11.00am-5.00pm and for traditional Sunday lunches from 12.30pm-4.00pm. Please contact the restaurant directly for details on menus and prices.

The Belfast Zoo is situated on a 55-acre site to the north of Belfast with panoramic views over the city and the lough below. This modern world-class Zoo acts as a safe haven for more than 160 species of rare and endangered animals, housed in award winning enclosures which replicate their natural environments. The primate trail, gorilla and chimpanzee enclosures, free-flight aviary, and giraffe housing are all outstanding examples of modern zoo-keeping.

Belfast Zoo has established an international reputation for its successes in breeding, particularly with endangered species. Its most notable recent successes have been the birth of a baby gorilla (only the second to be born in Ireland) and a baby elephant in 1997. Four baby giraffes have been bred successfully at the Zoo.

The Zoo is constantly developing, and among one of its most impressive attractions are pens which enable visitors to look at sea lions and penguins beneath the surface of the water. Land-based species include bears and marmosets. More recent additions to the Zoo family are Barbary lions, maned wolves, barn owls and Cape porcupines. The Belfast Zoo is one of the city's most popular family attractions, and although visitors should be prepared for a climb, the results are worth the effort.

Where is it?
City of Belfast Zoological Gardens
Antrim Road
Belfast BT36 7PN

Who do I contact?
Tel: 028 9077 6277
Fax: 028 9037 0578
Website: www.belfastzoo.co.uk

What do I need to know?
The Zoo is open every day from 10.00am (except Christmas Day and Boxing Day when it is closed). From 1st April until 30th September, the last admission is 5.00pm with the Zoo closing at 7.00pm. From 1st October until 31st March the last admission is at 2.30pm with the Zoo closing at 4.00pm. The Zoovenir Shop has a large range of souvenirs and animal themed gifts and closes 30 minutes after the last admission. The Restaurant closes at 5.30pm during the summer months and 3.30pm during the winter. The Zoo also has a children's playground, disabled access to all facilities and free parking. For information about forthcoming events, please visit the website.

CITY HALL

The City Hall, situated at Donegall Square in the heart of Belfast, is the seat of local government and also one of the most handsome buildings in the British Isles. It was here that local men signed the Ulster Covenant in their own blood in 1912 to prevent Home Rule coming to the North; and it was here that in 1921 King George V opened the first Northern Ireland Parliament with a poignant but unfulfilled plea for peace.

The City Hall was built from Portland Stone and completed in 1906, when Belfast was one of the greatest cities in the British Empire. It then had the greatest shipyard, ropeworks, tobacco factory, linen spinning mill, dry dock and tea machinery works in the world.

The City Hall exudes an air of Victorian grandeur, even if the architect Sir Brumwell Thomas reputedly had to chase the Corporation for his fee. However, an imperious statue of Queen Victoria herself outside the front entrance would have been assurance enough of Royal approval of such a stately pile in the Classical Renaissance style. While the exterior is indeed striking, the interior is equally impressive with its marble Entrance Hall and Grand Staircase, its Whispering Gallery, the Council Chamber and vast Great Hall, with stained-glass windows and a vaulted ceiling. There are many memorials, pictures and portraits – including those of very different Lord Mayors – which tell the colourful and often turbulent story of the city.

The City Hall grounds also relate an interesting story, and include the statues of Sir Edward Harland, one of the co-founders of the Belfast shipyard. Not far away, sadly, is a somewhat subdued white-marble figure commemorating the disastrous loss of the famous vessel *Titanic* which was built in Belfast.

On the other side of the City Hall there is an elaborate memorial to a dashing local nobleman, a former Marquis of Dufferin who at various times was Governor-General of Canada, British Ambassador to Moscow, and Viceroy of India. His statue embodying the height of British imperialism was unveiled in 1906, the same year in which the City Hall was completed. Visitors who want to trace the broad history of Belfast should spend some time at the City Hall.

Where is it?
City Hall
Donegall Square
Belfast BT1 5GS

Who do I contact?
Tel: 028 9027 0456
Fax: 028 9031 5252
Textphone: 028 9027 0405 (for the hard of hearing, calls to this number must be made from a Textphone)

What do I need to know?
Public and Private Group Tours available. Please contact 028 9027 0456 for further information. Giftware can be purchased from Monday to Fridays from 9.30am-4.00pm. Disabled ramps front and rear and lifts are available to all floors. There are also disabled toilets and automatic door openers. Staff are trained in Sign Language (BSL).

BELFAST

The Crown Liquor Saloon (popularly known as 'The Crown Bar') is one of the most ornate hostelries in the British Isles. It is lavishly decorated inside, and was once described by a former Poet Laureate Sir John Betjeman as "a many-coloured cavern."

This elaborate example of a high-Victorian public house was featured in the 1946 classic thriller *Odd Man Out*, which starred James Mason as a gunman on the run in Belfast. It was directed by Carol Reed and featured the Irish actor Cyril Cusack, as well as Belfast's own playwright and actor Joseph Tomelty. It is likely that both men would have known 'The Crown Bar' from personal experience.

It is said that the first owner was an ardent Irish nationalist and his wife was an Ulster unionist. It is believed that she insisted on naming it 'The Crown' but that he made his own mark by depicting a crown on the mosaic outside the entrance – so that visitors would walk all over it!

Whatever the truth, or otherwise, of this very Irish story, 'The Crown' still serves good beer and draught Guinness, and its distinctive wooden snugs still provide privacy in the modern world of "open-plan" design. A visit to 'The Crown' is a must for all who want to sample some of the atmosphere and true flavour of Belfast.

Where is it?
46 Great Victoria Street
Belfast BT2 7BA

Who do I contact?
Tel: 028 9027 9901
Email: info@crownbar.com
Website: www.ntni.org.uk *AND*
          www.thecrownbar.com

What do I need to know?
Open all year from Monday to Saturday from 11.30am-11.00pm. Sunday from 12.30pm-10.00pm. Last admission 30 minutes before closing.

DUNDONALD INTERNATIONAL ICE BOWL AND PIRATES ADVENTURE GOLF

Dundonald International Ice Bowl can accommodate more than 1000 seated spectators at ice events. It is an important attraction, which provides excellent individual, group and family entertainment. It is Ireland's only large Olympic-sized rink, and it hosts a wide variety of activities. Since it was opened in the 1980s, it has attracted some six million visitors.

Activities include music concerts and other events, as well as lessons on ice-skating and ice hockey. The rink can accommodate some 1,500 skaters daily. It is also the training-ground for the popular Belfast Giants professional team: ice hockey continues as one of the fastest-growing spectator sports in Northern Ireland.

As well as offering ice-skating, the Ice Bowl features 30 lanes of computerised tenpin bowling, and an indoor adventure playground with an 'Indiana Jones' theme. Another recent addition to the site is Pirates Adventure Golf. This is a Florida-style adventure golf complex which is the first of its kind in Ireland and features waterfalls, fountains and a fully rigged Pirate Schooner. You can even play at night as the course is floodlit.

Where is it?
111 Old Dundonald Road
Dundonald
Belfast BT16 0XT

Who do I contact?
Tel: 028 9080 9100
Website: www.theicebowl.com

For further information on Pirates Adventure Golf please contact:
Tel: 028 9048 0220
Email: info@piratesadventuregolf.com
Website: www.piratesadventuregolf.com

What do I need to know?
Open daily from 10.00am –10.00pm daily. Times for various activities can vary – please ring for further details. Alaska Sports Café. Party packages are available for children of 11 and under – please telephone 028 9129 9123 for further details.

The Linen Hall Library, situated in the city centre just across the street from the City Hall, was established in 1788. It is Belfast's oldest library, with a wealth of history from many different sources. Like many other local institutions, it has survived through troubled times, and it has a unique Irish and Local Studies Collection which reflects the complexity of the historical and cultural background of the region. This includes early local books, and some 250,000 items in the Northern Ireland Political Collection. There is an extensive General Lending Collection, as well as a Theatre and Performing Arts Archive and other sections featuring the Languages of Ulster, Genealogy and Heraldry.

The Linen Hall is a major information centre for those who want to know more about the Province and its history, and it is an authoritative research base for many well-known authors, journalists and broadcasters. The Library runs a regular series of cultural and other events each year, which underline its reputation as an important resource for the creative life of the community. There is also a good Coffee House, a collection of prints and gifts for sale, and a wide range of newspapers and magazines in the Members' Room.

Where is it?
17 Donegall Square North
Belfast BT1 5GB

Who do I contact?
Tel: 028 9032 1707
Fax: 028 9043 8586
Email: info@linenhall.com
Website: www.linenhall.com

What do I need to know?
The Library is open to non-members Monday to Friday from 9.30am-5.30pm and on Saturday from 9.30am-1.00pm. Closed Sundays. A free tour is given on Wednesday mornings at 11.30am which lasts for around 45 minutes. An on-line shopping service is available through the website.

QUEEN'S UNIVERSITY – VISITORS' CENTRE AND NAUGHTON GALLERY

Queen's University, in the leafy southern suburbs, is the premier seat of learning in Northern Ireland, and one of the best centres of third-level education in the British Isles. It was established in 1845 as one of the three 'Queen's Colleges' in Ireland – the others being situated in Cork and Galway. The 'Queen's College' in Belfast was opened in 1849, and it was host in August of that year to the young Queen Victoria and her Consort Prince Albert, as part of a State Visit to Ireland. The famous front building was designed by the Belfast architect Sir Charles Lanyon. It is still referred to as 'the Lanyon', and in daylight or in floodlight it is one of the most beautiful buildings in Ireland, north and south.

The University's famous *alumni* include the Nobel Laureates Seamus Heaney the poet, and the former Unionist leader David Trimble, as well as Irish President Mary McAleese. The institution has also played a major role in community life, and was a pivotal force in the development of the successful Belfast Festival and also the ground-breaking Queen's Film Theatre.

Queen's is set in its own attractively landscaped grounds, and it has an excellent modern Visitors' Centre and Naughton Gallery, both of which are situated near the front entrance. The atmosphere at Queen's is particularly lively during term time, but during vacations – and especially in summer – the beautiful inner quadrangle mirrors the peace of an Oxbridge College.

Where is it?
Queen's University Belfast
Lanyon Building
University Road
Belfast BT7 1NN

Who do I contact?
Naughton Gallery:
Tel: 028 9097 3580
Email: art@naughtongallery.org
Website: www.naughtongallery.org

Queen's Visitors' Centre
Tel: 028 9097 5252
Email: visitors.centre@qub.ac.uk
Website: www.qub.ac.uk

What do I need to know?

The gallery is open Monday to Saturday from 11.00am-4.00pm. Queen's Visitors' Centre is open Monday to Friday from 10.00am-4.00pm and on Saturday (May-September only) from 10.00am-4.00pm. Guided group tours of the campus are available by arrangement with the Visitors' Centre. Please contact the Visitors' Centre directly for further information. Wheelchair access.

ST ANNE'S CATHEDRAL

St Anne's Cathedral is on the site of Belfast's first Church of Ireland building, which was also called St Anne's. The first church on this site dated from 1776 and was founded by the Marquis of Donegall. It was later demolished in 1903. The foundation stone for St Anne's Cathedral was laid in 1899 by the Countess of Shaftesbury. Today St Anne's plays an important role in the life of the city.

The Cathedral, with its Hiberno-Romanesque Nave, was erected in stages. The West Font was dedicated to those who fought and died in World War I and was not finished until 1927. The Cathedral itself was finally completed in 1981 when the North Transept finished, with the Chapel of the Royal Irish Rangers and the Royal Irish Regiment. A Chapel of Unity was consecrated in 1973.

St Anne's Cathedral is noted for its beautiful architecture, stained glass windows and mosaics. It is also home to the largest Celtic cross in Ireland and appropriately for a congregation noted for its fine music, the Cathedral contains the largest pipe organ in Northern Ireland. St Anne's serves as a major worship centre for State, civic and community events. It has close ties with St Peter's Roman Catholic Pro-Cathedral in West Belfast. Each Christmas St Anne's stages a 'Black Santa' sit-out, which raises huge sums for local and overseas charities.

Where is it?
Donegall Street
Belfast BT1 2HB

Who do I contact?
Tel: 028 9032 8332
Email: admin@belfastcathedral.org
Website: www.belfastcathedral.org

What do I need to know?
The Cathedral is open to visitors from Monday to Saturday 10.00am-4.00pm. Open on Sunday before and after services. Guided tours by prior arrangement. Parking is available free of charge on Sundays for those attending worship. Parking is also available on Saturdays for a small fee.

ULSTER FOLK AND TRANSPORT MUSEUM

The Ulster Folk and Transport Museum is one of the best of its kind in the world, and provides an important background to the living history of the Province and its people.

The Folk Museum has more than 60 acres of exhibits and artefacts from the rural history of Ulster. These include former homesteads, churches and other buildings which have helped to underline the unique character and the way of life of the people of succeeding generations. The Folk Museum has been evolving since the 1950s and is set in the graceful Cultra Manor estate outside Belfast.

The Transport Museum based nearby has a comprehensive collection of exhibits that trace the history of transportation in the Province since early times. It includes examples of Northern Ireland's outstanding engineering and aeronautical successes, including the Sunderland flying-boat and the Shorts Skyvan.

There is also an example of an early Model-T Ford car, and the exotic but ill-fated De Lorean gull-wing DMC car. The tasteful setting of the Ulster Folk and Transport Museum provides an excellent and informative focus for those who wish to know more about the Province, and there is enough in each to fill a visit of several hours.

Where is it?
Cultra
Holywood
Co. Down BT18 0EU

Who do I contact?
Tel: 028 9042 8428
Website: www.uftm.org.uk

What do I need to know?

The Museum opens at 10.00am from Monday to Saturday and from 11.00am on Sunday. Closing times depend on the time of year. The museum is open every day throughout the year but is closed over Christmas. Please contact for details if you plan to visit at this time. Visitors can buy a combined ticket for both museum locations, or a single ticket for either. There is no entry charge for disabled visitors and most (but not all) areas are fully accessible to wheelchair users. Disabled toilets are available. There are tearooms and picnic areas on site but portable barbecues are not permitted. A Sunday Carvery lunch is held from September-July. Both museum sites have giftshops.

ULSTER MUSEUM

The Ulster Museum has a wide range of exhibits, including some 2,000 objects from Ancient Egypt. This includes the case and mummy of a woman named Takabuti. The Museum also has a fine collection of gold and silver jewellery, coins and other artefacts from the Spanish Armada vessel *Girona* which sank amid severe storms off the Causeway Coast in 1588.

The Ulster Museum has a good art gallery, and regularly stages special exhibitions, including in recent years works by outstanding Irish artists such as Sir John Lavery and his contemporaries. The Museum also has an important

Engineering Hall and Textile Gallery, featuring Belfast's golden years of engineering, and its once-flourishing textile and linen trades.

The Ulster Museum has other important displays featuring Irish archaeology, ethnography, history and natural sciences. There is much to attract visitors of all ages. The facilities include a good café, which overlooks the historic Friar's Bush graveyard, where some of Belfast's most noted citizens were buried.

It is important to note, however, that the Ulster Museum is scheduled to close for two years from late 2006 for major renovations.

Where is it?
Botanic Gardens
Belfast BT9 5AB

Who do I contact?
Tel: 028 9038 3000
Website: www.ulstermuseum.org.uk

What do I need to know?
The normal opening hours: Monday to Friday from 10.00am-5.00pm and on Saturday from 1.00pm-5.00pm and on Sunday from 2.00pm-5.00pm. Disabled visitors can park within the grounds if prior notice is given on 028 9038 3042. There is a disabled toilet and lift access to all floors. Guide dogs welcome. The museum has its own giftshop and café. Food and drinks cannot be consumed in the galleries. School or youth groups can book their visit through the Education Services Department on 028 9038 3030. PLEASE NOTE! The Ulster Museum is closed for two years from late 2006 for renovation.

INDEX